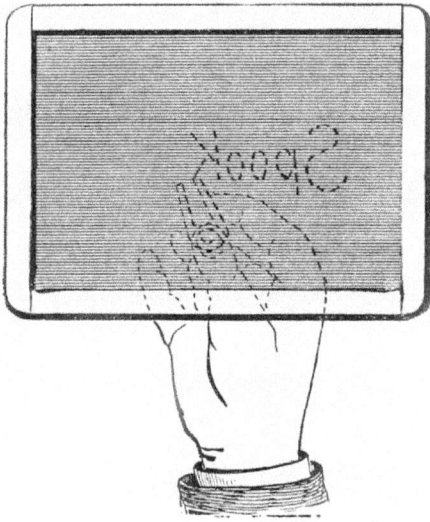

SPIRIT SLATE WRITING

AND

KINDRED PHENOMENA

BY

WILLIAM E. ROBINSON

Cur*i*ous

PUBLICATIONS

New York

Published by Curious Publications.
curiouspublications.com
Copyright © 2020

First published in 1898 by Munn & Company.

Cabinet card photo of William E. Robinson courtesy of Potter & Potter
Auctions. Images in the introduction come from the public domain.

ISBN-13: 978-0-9862393-6-6

Printed and bound in the United States of America.

A NOTE ON THE TEXT

The book you now hold was originally published in 1898 by William E. Robinson, a magician who would later become more famous under his stage name, Chung Ling Soo. The introduction that's been added for this edition was written seven years later by magician, magic historian, and critic of Spiritualism, Henry Ridgely Evans. Just as Robinson exposed how mediums worked their brand of magic from beyond the veil, Evans's words offer a peek behind the curtain to discover who Robinson was, and how a few of his own illusions worked.

William E. Robinson, circa 1895.

INTRODUCTION

By Henry Ridgely Evans
Originally published in "Some Magicians I Have Met."
The Open Court, a Quarterly Magazine, August 1905.

William E. Robinson for years acted as Alexander Herrmann's stage manager and machinist. He is a devotee of the magic art, a collector of rare books on legerdemain, and the inventor of many ingenious sleights, tricks, and illusions. When not employed at the theatre, he spends his time haunting the second-hand bookstores, searching for literature on his favorite hobby. He has found time to write a profoundly interesting brochure called Spirit Slate Writing, published by the Scientific American Company. After reading this work, I cannot see how any sane person can credit the reality of "independent slate-writing." It is a mere juggling trick.

Robinson was born in New York City, April 2, 1861, and received a common school education. He started life as "a worker in brass and other metals," but he abandoned the profession of Tubal Cain for conjuring. After the death of Herrmann, Robinson went as assistant to Leon Herrmann for several seasons, and then started out to astonish the natives on his own account, but without any appreciable success. Just about this time there came to the United States a Chinese conjurer named Ching Ling Foo, with a repertoire of Oriental tricks. One of them was the production of a huge bowl of water from a table cloth, followed by live pigeons and ducks, and last but

INTRODUCTION

not least a little almond-eyed Celestial, his son. This was but a replica of the trick which Philippe learned from the Chinese many years ago. Foo's performances drew crowds to the theatres. It was the novelty of the thing that caught the public fancy. In reality, the Mongolian's magic was not to be compared with that of Herrmann, Kellar, or Goldin. Beneath the folds of a Chinese robe one may conceal almost anything, ranging in size from a bed post to a cannon ball. When Foo's manager boastfully advertised to forfeit $500, if any American could fathom or duplicate any of the Celestials tricks, "Billy" Robinson came forward and accepted the challenge. But nothing came of it. Foo's impressario "backed water," to use a boating phrase. Robinson was so taken with Ching Ling Foo's act that he decided to give similar séances, disguising himself as a Chinaman. Under the name of Chung Ling Soo he went to England accompanied by his wife and a genuine Chinese acrobat. He opened at the Empire Theatre, and not only reproduced Foo's best tricks but added others of his own, equally as marvelous. His success was instantaneous. Theatrical London went wild over the celebrated Chinese wizard, and gold began to flow into the coffers of the Robinson menage. So well was the secret kept that for months no one, except the attachés of the theatre, knew that Chung Ling Soo was a Yankee and not a genuine Chinaman. The make-up of himself and wife was perfect. Robinson even had the audacity to grant interviews to newspaper reporters. He usually held these receptions at his lodgings where he had an apartment fitted up à la Chinois; the walls hung with silken drapery embroidered with grotesque dragons. The place was dimly lit by Chinese lanterns. Propped up on silken cushions, the "Yankee Celestial" with his face like a finely painted mask, sipped his real oolong and laughed in his capacious sleeves at the credulity of the journalistic hacks. He gave his opinions on the "Boxer" trouble, speaking a kind of gibberish which the previously tutored Chinese acrobat pretended to interpret into English. Gradually it leaked out in theatrical circles that Chung Ling Soo was a Yankee, but this information never came to the public ear generally.

At the close of the "Boxer" uprising the real Ching Ling Foo had returned to his beloved Flowery Kingdom, loaded down with bags full of dollars extracted from the pockets of the "Foreign Devils," yclept Americans. Under his own vine and bamboo tree he proceeded to enjoy life like a regular Chinese gentleman; to burn joss sticks to the memory of his ancestors, and study the maxims of Confucius. But the longing for other worlds to conquer with his magic overcame him, and so in the year 1904 he went to England. Great was his

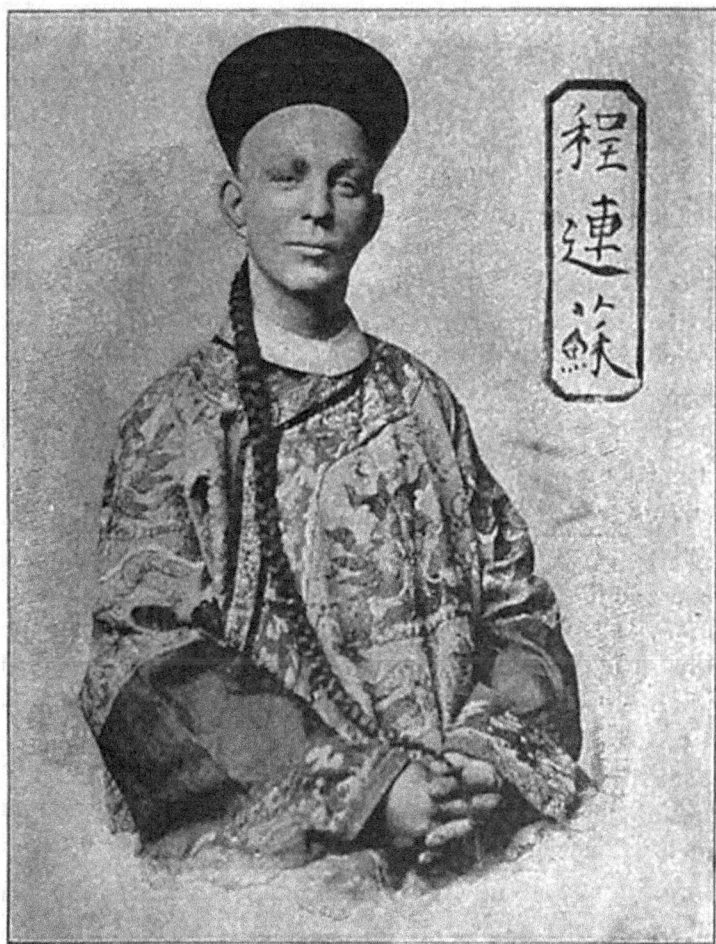

William E. Robinson as Chung Ling Soo

astonishment to find that a pretended Mongolian had preceded him and stolen all of his thunder. In January 1905, Robinson was playing at the Hippodrome, London, and Ching Ling Foo at the Empire.

There was great rivalry between them. The result was that Foo challenged Soo to a grand trial of strength, the articles of which appeared in the Weekly Despatch: "I offer £1,000 if Chung Ling Soo, now appearing at the Hippodrome, can do ten out of the twenty of my tricks, or if I fail to do any one of his feats."

A meeting was arranged to take place at the Despatch office, on January 7, 1905, at 11 A. M. The challenged man, "Billy" Robinson alias Chung Ling Soo rode up to the newspaper office in his big red automobile, accompanied by his manager and assistants. He was dressed like a mandarin. The acrobat held over his master's head a gorgeous Chinese umbrella. Robinson gave an exhibition of his skill before a committee of newspaper men and theatrical managers. Foo came not. The next day arrived a letter from Ching Ling Foo's impressario saying that the Mongolian magician would only consent to compete against his rival on the following condition: "That Chung Ling Soo first prove before members of the Chinese Legation that he is a Chinaman." This was whipping the Devil (or shall I say Dragon) around the stump. The original challenge had made no condition as to the nationality of the performers.

The Despatch said: "The destination of the challenge money remains in abeyance, and the questions arise: 'Did Foo fool Soo? And can Soo sue Foo?'"

The merits of this interesting mix-up are thus summed up by Mr. John N. Hilliard, in an editorial published in the Sphinx, Kansas City, Mo., March 15, 1905:

"While we do not take the controversy with undue seriousness, there is an ethical aspect in the case, however, that invites discussion. In commenting disparagingly on the professional ability of the Chinese conjurer, in belittling his originality and his achievements in the magic arts, Mr. Robinson (Chung Ling Soo) is really throwing stones at his own crystal dwelling place. Despite the glowing presentments of his press agent, one single naked truth shines out as clearly as a frosty star in a turquoise sky. It is violating no confidence to assert that had it not been for Ching Ling Foo, the professional status of Mr. William E. Robinson, masquerading as a Chinaman, and adopting the sobriquet of 'Chung Ling Soo,' would be more or less of a negative quantity to-day. Ching Ling Foo, the genuine Chinaman, is indisputably the originator, so far as the Western hemisphere is concerned, at least, of this peculiar act, and Robinson is merely an imitator. Robinson is shrewd and has a 'head for business.' He doubtless realizes, as well as his critics, that in the dress of the modern magician, he would not be unqualifiedly successful, despite his skill with cards and coins and his soul edge of the art. The success of Ching Ling Foo in this country was his opportunity. Adopting the dress and make-up of a Mongolian, and appropriating the leading features of Ching's act, he went to Europe, where the act was a novelty, and scored a great success. Of course, from a utilitarian point of view, this success is legitimate; but in the light of what the American magician really owes to the great Chinese conjurer, it is ridiculous for Robinson to pose as the original Chinese magician and for him to say that Ching Ling Foo is a performer of the streets, while he is the 'court magician to the Empress Dowager.' This may be good showmanship, but it is not fair play. The devil himself is entitled to his due; and, the question of merit aside, the indubitable fact remains that it is Ching Ling Foo, who is the 'original Chinese magician,' while 'Chung Ling Soo' is an imitator of his act and a usurper in the Oriental kingdom. But outside of the ethical nature of the controversy, we refuse to take it seriously."

Robinson is the inventor of the fever stage illusion "Gone," which Hermann exhibited, and which still forms one of the principal specialties of Kellar. I am indebted to my friend, Henry V. A. Parsell, for an accurate description of the trick, as at present worked by Mr. Kellar.

"At the rise of the curtain the stage is seen to have its rear part concealed by a second curtain and drapery which, being drawn up, discloses a substantial framework. This framework, at the first glance, gives one the impression that it is that horrible instrument of death, the guillotine. As will be seen, it consists simply of two uprights, with a bar across the top and another a little below the middle. Just below the centre bar is a windlass, the two ropes of which pass through two pulleys fixed to the top bar. The machine stands out boldly against a black background, the distance from which is indeterminate.

"After the introduction of the fair maiden 'who is to be gone,' an ordinary-looking bent wood chair is shown. The chair is then placed on the stage behind the framework, and by means of snap hooks, the two ropes from the windlass are attached to the side of the chair. The maiden is now seated in the chair and her skirt adjusted that it may not hang too low.

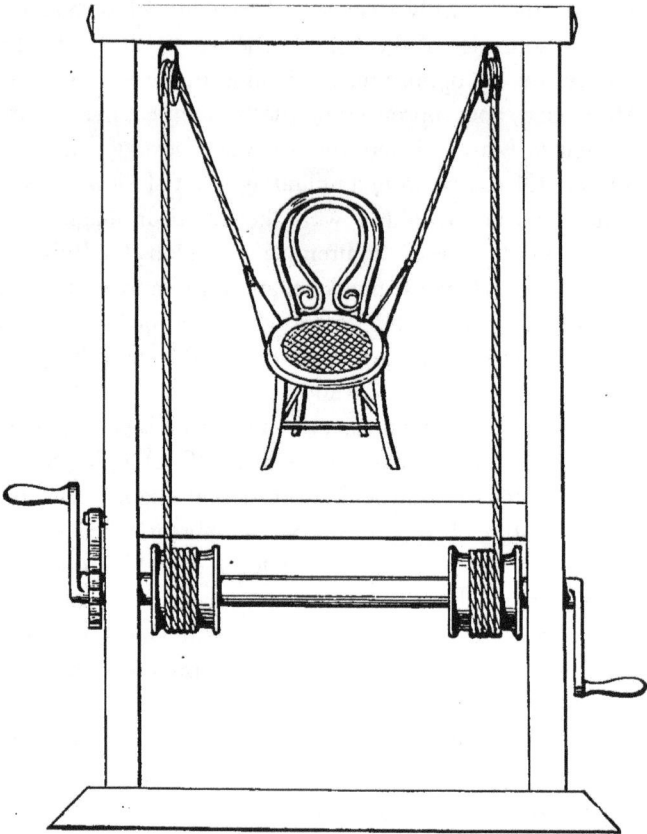

"GONE." Robinson's illusion.

"A couple of assistants now work the windlass and elevate the chair and its occupant until they are well above the middle cross bar. One assistant then retires, the other remains with one hand resting against the side of the framework. The performer fires his pistol thrice, upon which the maiden vanishes and the fragments of the chair fall to the ground. The illusion is produced by a black curtain which lies concealed behind the middle cross bar. When the pistol is fired, the assistant, whose hand is on the frame, presses a spring which releases this black curtain which is instantly drawn up in front of the suspended girl. At this same moment the girl undoes a couple of catches which allows the main part of the chair to drop. She, meanwhile, being seated on a false chair-bottom to which the ropes are attached."

As originally devised by Mr. Robinson, the illusion was based upon the Pepper ghost-show, as will be seen in the illustration. Between the cross-bars of a slanting frame was a sheet of plate glass which, being invisible, left the lady on the chair in full view as long as the light fell upon her. A screen of the same color as the background was concealed above the curtain and placed at such an angle as to allow its reflection to pass out to the audience. The firing of the pistol was the signal for the assistant to turn a switch. The lady was then veiled in relative darkness while the screen was illuminated and its reflection on the plate-glass concealed her from sight. Carrying around the country a big sheet of plate glass is not only an expensive luxury but a risky one, so the illusion was simplified in the manner described by Mr. Parsell.

"The Spiritualistic Séance."

SPIRIT SLATE WRITING

AND

KINDRED PHENOMENA

BY

WILLIAM E. ROBINSON

Assistant to the late Herrmann

———————

SIXTY-SIX ILLUSTRATIONS

———————

MUNN & COMPANY
SCIENTIFIC AMERICAN OFFICE
NEW YORK CITY

1898

PREFACE.

THE author of the present volume is not an opponent of spiritualism—on the contrary, he was brought up from childhood in this belief; and though, at the present writing, he does not acknowledge the truth of its teachings, nevertheless he respects the feelings of those who are honest in their convictions. At the same time he confidently believes that all rational persons, spiritualists as well as others, will heartily indorse this endeavor to explain the methods of those who, under the mask of mediumship, and possessing all the artifices of the charlatan, victimize those seeking knowledge of their loved ones who have passed away. As a great New York lawyer once said, it was not spiritualism he was fighting, but fraud under the guise of spiritualism.

Owing to the fact that the author has for many years been engaged in the practice of the profession of magic, both as a prestidigitateur and designer of stage illusions for the late Alexander Herrmann, and has also been associated with Prof. Kellar, he feels that he is fitted to treat of clever tricks used by mediums. He has attended hundreds of séances both at home and abroad, and the present volume is the fruit of his studies.

Some of the means of working these slate tests may appear simple and impossible of deceiving, but in the hands of the medium they are entirely successful. It should be remembered it is not so much the apparatus employed as it is the shrewd, cunning, ever-observing sharper using it. The devices and methods employed by slate writing frauds seem innumerable. No sooner are they caught and exposed while employing one system than they immediately set their wits to work and evolve an entirely different idea. It is almost impossible at the first sitting with a slate writing medium to know what method he will employ, and should you, after the sitting, go away with the idea that you have discovered his method of operation and come a second time ready to expose him, you may be sadly disappointed, for the medium will undoubtedly lead you to believe he is going to use his former method, and so mislead you. He accomplishes his test by another method, while you are on the lookout for something entirely different. The great success of the medium is in disarming the suspicions of the skeptic, and at that very moment the trick is done. Slate writing is of course the great standby of mediums, but there are many other tricks which they employ which are described in the present volume.

The publishers have added a chapter on "Miscellaneous Tricks" which may serve as a supplement to their "Magic: Stage Illusions and Scientific Diversions, Including Trick Photography," which has already obtained an enviable position in the literature of magic, and has been even translated into Swedish. These tricks are by Mr. W. B. Caulk and the author.

NEW YORK, November, 1898.

TABLE OF CONTENTS.

SPIRIT SLATE WRITING

AND

KINDRED PHENOMENA.

CHAPTER I.

THE SINGLE SLATE.

There has probably been nothing that has made more converts to spiritualism than the much talked of "Slate Writing Test," and if we are to believe some of the stories told of the writings mysteriously obtained on slates, under what is known as "severe test conditions," that preclude, beyond any possible doubt, any form of deception or trickery, one would think that the day of miracles had certainly returned; but we must not believe half we hear nor all that we see, for the chances are that just as you are about to attribute some unaccountable spirit phenomena to an unseen power, something turns up to show that you have been tricked by a clever device which is absurd in its simplicity.

There are a large number of methods of producing slate writing, but the writer will describe a few which will be sufficient to give an idea of the working of slate tests in general. First we have the ordinary one in which the writing is placed on the slate beforehand, and then hidden from view by a flap or loose piece of slate. (Fig. 1.) After both sides of the slate have been cleaned, the false flap is dropped on the table, the side which is then uppermost being covered with cloth similar to the table top, where it will remain unnoticed, or the flap is allowed to fall into a second slate with which the first is covered. In the latter case no cloth is pasted on the flap. Sometimes the flap is covered with a piece of newspaper and is allowed to drop into a newspaper lying on the table, then the newspaper containing the flap is carelessly removed, thus doing away with any trace of trickery.

Fig. 1. Ordinary Slate with Flap.

Another way of utilizing the false flap is as follows: The writing is not placed beforehand on the slate, but on the flap, which, as before, is covered with the same material as the table top. This is lying on the table writing downward. The slate is handed around for inspection, and, on being returned to the performer, he stands at the table and cleans the slate on one side, then turns it over and cleans the other. As he does so he lifts the flap into the slate. The flap is held in firmly by an edging of thin pure sheet rubber cemented on the flap between the slate and the cloth covering of the slate. This grips the wooden sides of the frame hard enough to prevent the false piece from tumbling out accidentally.

We now come to another style, wherein a slate is cleaned on both sides, and, while held in the hand facing the audience, becomes suddenly covered with writing, and the slate is immediately given for inspection. The writing is on the slate previous to the cleaning, and is hidden from view by a flap of slate colored silk, held firmly in place by a pellet of wax in each of the corners of the silk. Attached to this silk flap or covering (at the end that is nearest to the performer's sleeve) is a stout cord or string, which is also made fast to a strap around the wrist of the hand opposite to that holding the slate. If the arms are now extended their full length, the piece of silk covering will leave the slate and pass rapidly up the sleeve out of the way, and thus leave the writing exposed to view. (Fig. 2.) The slate is found to be still a little damp from the cleaning with the sponge and water it had been given previously. This is easily accounted for. The water from the sponge penetrates just enough through the cloth to dampen the slate.

Fig. 2. Removing the Silk from the Face of the Slate.

There is still another slate on which we can make the writing appear suddenly. It is composed of a wooden frame, such as all wooden-edged slates have, but the slate itself is a sham. It is a piece of cloth painted with a kind of paint known as liquid, or silicate slating, which, when dry and hard, is similar to the real article. This cloth is twice the length of the slate and just the exact width. The two ends of the cloth are united with cement, so as to make an endless piece or loop. There is a small rod or roller in both the top and bottom pieces of the frame, the ends being made hollow to receive them. Over these rollers runs the cloth, stretched firmly and tightly. Just where the cloth is joined or cemented is a little black button, or stud of hard rubber or leather. This allows the cloth to be pushed up and down, bringing the back to the front; and by doing so quickly, the writing which is written on the cloth at the rear of the frame is made to come to the front in plain view. (Fig. 3.)

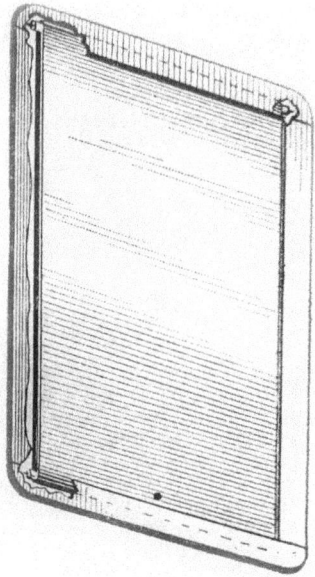

Fig. 3. The Endless Band
Silicate Trick Slate.

Still another idea in a single slate is as follows: An ordinary looking slate is given out for examination, and, on its being returned to the medium, he takes his handkerchief and cleans or brushes both sides of the slate with it; and, upon again showing that side of the slate first cleaned, it is found covered with writing apparently done with chalk. The following is the simple explanation of it: Take a small camel's hair brush and dip it in urine or onion juice, and with it write or trace on the slate whatever you desire, and when it becomes dry, or nearly so, the slate can be given for examination without fear of detection.

The handkerchief the performer uses to clean the slate with is lightly sprinkled with powdered chalk. He makes believe to clean the one side devoid of preparation, but the side containing the invisible writing is gently rubbed with the handkerchief, not too hard just enough to let the powdered chalk fall on the urine or onion juice, where it leaves a mark not unlike a chalk mark.

It will not be out of place to describe a trick by which writing is produced upon an ordinary china plate by a somewhat similar means. The plate is examined and cleaned with a borrowed handkerchief, and then the performer requests the loan of a pinch of snuff, or uses a little sand or dust, which he places on the plate. He now commences to move the plate around in circles, and while doing so the snuff or sand is seen to gradually form itself into writing. The explanation is simple—whatever writing you desire to appear on the plate is placed beforehand on it. It is done with a camel's hair brush dipped in the white of an egg and allowed to become dry before being handed around for inspection. As the performer cleans the plate he breathes on both sides of it, as if to give it moisture enough to help take off any dirt that might be thereon when rubbed with the handkerchief. In breathing on the front of the plate containing the writing done with the white of the egg, he moistens the writing enough to make the snuff or sand, as the case may be, adhere to it. Of course, in cleaning the front of the plate, care must be taken not to brush or disturb the invisible writing.

It may not be amiss to also mention another method of producing writing, employed by mediums to obtain a message on a blank piece of paper which has been placed between two slates, which are held by the medium in his hand, high above his head, and, on afterwards taking the slate apart, the paper is covered with writing. This again calls into use the extra or false flap. (Fig. 1.) A piece of paper with writing on it is placed face downward on one of the slates and covered with the false flap. It then looks like an ordinary slate. On this is placed the plain piece of paper, and over this is laid the second slate. The slates are now held up in plain view of the audience, and on being lowered to the table they are turned over, thus bringing the blank piece of paper under the false flap and the one with the writing on it on the top of the flap, which has fallen from the slate, which is now the top, but originally the bottom one, on or into the under one, and, of course, on the removal of the present top slate, the writing is found on what is supposed to be the original blank paper.

If the paper is to have a private mark put on it by an observer, so as to prove the writing really does appear on that identical piece of paper, the operation is varied as follows: The false flap is done away with, and the paper, which is furnished by the medium, has written on it the desired communication with ink, which is made visible and brought out black by means of heat. For the invisible ink you can use sulphuric acid, very much diluted, so as not to destroy the paper.

Fig. 4. False Table for Developing Communications
Written with Sympathetic Ink.

The necessary heat is obtained in the following manner: The table (Fig. 4) on which the slates are resting is hollow, and has concealed in it a spirit lamp filled with alcohol. This lamp sits directly under a trap in the table top, which is covered underneath for safety with sheet iron, so it will not catch fire. When the slates are placed on the table they are laid over the little trap door, which, in conjuring parlance, is known as a "trap." This is now opened, and the slates allowed to become well heated and the trap then closed, and the prepared paper, upon coming in contact with the hot slate, is thus covered with writing.

Another medium employed a somewhat similar method, only the paper in this case was placed in a glass vial (Fig. 5) which had been lying on the iron trap door. The medium's hand covered the vial, which was corked and sealed, while the writing was making its appearance. You can also produce writing on the paper in the vial without resorting to the use of heat by using a vial that has been washed out with ammonia and kept well corked, and writing on the paper with a weak solution of copper sulphate, which is invisible until the paper is placed in the vial, when the two chemicals produce writing in blue. Still another message is produced as follows: The writing is done with iron sulphate on blank cards. Of course this is invisible. These cards are placed in envelopes and sealed up. Upon opening the envelopes shortly afterward the cards are covered with the writing which was before invisible, but is brought out by a solution of nut galls with which the inside of the envelopes had been slightly moistened.

Fig. 5. The Development of Spirit Writing.

The subject of sympathetic inks is such an interesting one that we give thirty-seven formulas, which include all those which are liable to be used by the medium.

The solutions used should be so nearly colorless that the writing cannot be seen till the agent is applied to render it visible. Sympathetic inks are of three general classes.

Inks that Appear through Heat.

1. Write with a concentrated solution of caustic potash. The writing will appear when the paper is submitted to strong heat.

2. Write with a solution of ammonium hydrochlorate, in the proportion of 15 parts to 100. The writing will appear when the paper is heated by holding it over a stove or by passing a hot smoothing iron over it.

3. A weak solution of copper nitrate gives an invisible writing, which becomes red through heat.

4. A very dilute solution of copper perchloride gives invisible characters that become yellow through heat.

5. A slightly alcoholic solution of copper bromide gives perfectly invisible characters which are made apparent by a gentle heat, and which disappear again through cold.

6. Write upon rose colored paper with a solution of cobalt chloride. The invisible writing will become blue through heat, and will disappear on cooling.

7. Write with a solution of sulphuric acid. The characters will appear in black through heat. This ink has the disadvantage of destroying the paper. (See the caution given on page 12.)

8. Write with lemon, onion, leek, cabbage or artichoke juice. Characters written with these juices become very visible when the paper is heated.

9. Digest 1 oz. of zaffre, or cobalt oxide, at a gentle heat, with 4 oz. of nitro-muriatic acid till no more is dissolved, then add 1 oz. common salt and 16 oz. of water. If this be written with and the paper held to the fire, the writing becomes green, unless the cobalt should be quite

pure, in which case it will be blue. The addition of a little iron nitrate will then impart the property of becoming green. It is used in chemical landscapes for the foliage.

10. Put in a vial ½ oz. of distilled water, 1 drm. of potassium bromide and 1 drm. of pure copper sulphate. The solution is nearly colorless, but becomes brown when heated.

11. Nickel nitrate and nickel chloride in weak solution form an invisible ink, which becomes green by heating when the salt contains traces of cobalt, which usually is the case; when pure, it becomes yellow.

12. When the solution of acetate of protoxide of cobalt contains nickel or iron, the writing made by it will become green when heated; when it is pure and free from these metals, it becomes blue.

13. Milk makes a good invisible ink, and buttermilk answers the purpose better. It will not show if written with a clean new pen, and ironing with a hot flat iron is the best way of showing it up. All invisible inks will show on glazed paper; therefore unglazed paper should be used.

14. Burn flax so that it may be rather smoldered than burned to ashes, then grind it with a muller on a stone, putting a little alcohol to it, then mix it with a little gum water, and what you write, though it seem clear, may be rubbed or washed out.

15. Boil cobalt oxide in acetic acid. If a little common salt be added, the writing becomes green when heated, but with potassium nitrate it becomes a pale rose color.

16. A weak solution of mercury nitrate becomes black by heat.

Inks that Appear under the Influence of Light.

17. Gold chloride serves for forming characters that appear only as

long as the paper is exposed to daylight, say for an hour at least.

18. Write with a solution made by dissolving one part of silver nitrate in 1,000 parts of distilled water. When submitted to daylight, the writing appears of a slate color or tawny brown.

Inks Appearing through Reagents.

19. If writing be done with a solution of lead acetate in distilled water, the characters will appear in black upon passing a solution of an alkaline sulphide over the paper.

20. Characters written with a very weak solution of gold chloride will become dark brown upon passing a solution of tin perchloride over them.

21. Characters written with a solution of gallic acid in water will become black through a solution of iron sulphate and brown through the alkalies.

22. Upon writing on paper that contains but little sizing with a very clear solution of starch, and submitting the dry characters to the vapor of iodine, or passing over them a weak solution of potassium iodide, the writing becomes blue, and disappears under the action of a solution of sodium hyposulphite in the proportions of 1 to 1,000.

23. Characters written with a 10 per cent. solution of nitrate of protoxide of mercury become black when the paper is moistened with liquid ammonia, and gray through heat.

24. Characters written with a weak solution of the soluble platinum or iridium chloride become black when the paper is submitted to mercurial vapor. This ink may be used for marking linen. It is indelible.

25. C. Widemann communicates a new method of making an invisible ink to *Die Natur*. To make the writing or the drawing appear which

has been made upon paper with the ink, it is sufficient to dip it into water. On drying, the traces disappear again, and reappear by each succeeding immersion. The ink is made by intimately mixing linseed oil, 1 part; water of ammonia, 20 parts; water, 100 parts. The mixture must be agitated each time before the pen is dipped into it, as a little of the oil may separate and float on top, which would, of course, leave an oily stain upon the paper.

26. Write with a solution of potassium ferro-cyanide, develop by ressing over the dry, invisible characters a piece of blotting paper moistened with a solution of copper sulphate or of iron sulphate.

27. Write with pure dilute tincture of iron; develop with a blotter moistened with strong tea.

28. Writing with potassium iodide and starch becomes blue by the least trace of acid vapors in the atmosphere or by the presence of ozone. To make it, boil starch, and add a small quantity of potassium iodide in solution.

29. Copper sulphate in very dilute solution will produce an invisible writing, which will turn light blue by vapors of ammonia.

30. Soluble compounds of antimony will become red by hydrogen sulphide vapor.

31. Soluble compounds of arsenic and of tin peroxide will become yellow by the same vapor.

32. An acid solution of iron chloride is diluted till the writing is invisible when dry. This writing has the remarkable property of becoming red by sulphocyanide vapors (arising from the action of sulphuric acid on potassium sulphocyanide in a long necked flask), and it disappears by ammonia, and may alternately be made to appear and disappear by these two vapors.

33. Writing executed with rice water is visible when dry, but the char-

acters become blue by the application of iodine. This ink was much employed during the Indian mutiny.

34. Write with a solution of paraffin in benzol. When the solvent has evaporated, the paraffin is invisible, but becomes visible on being dusted with lampblack or powdered graphite, or smoking over a candle flame.

35. To Write Black Characters with Water.—Mix 10 parts nutgalls, 2½ parts calcined iron sulphate. Dry thoroughly, and reduce to fine powder. Rub this powder over the surface of the paper, and force nto the pores by powerful pressure, brush off the loose powder. A pen dipped in water will write black on paper thus treated.

36. To Write Blue Characters with Water.—Mix iron sesquisulphate and potassium ferrocyanide. Prepare the paper in the same manner as for writing black characters with water. Write with water, and the characters will appear blue.

37. To Produce Brown Writing with Water.—Mix copper sulphate and potassium ferrocyanide. Prepare the paper in the same manner as before. The characters written with water will be reddish brown.

Here is another trick calling for the use of sympathetic ink. A medium suggests a number of questions to write on a paper, one of which you select and write on a slip of paper furnished by the medium. Writing is done with pen and ink. You are requested to dry it with a blotter, and not to remove the blotter for a time, the medium says, so as to keep the paper in the dark, thus giving the "spirits" better conditions under which to work. After a while the blotter is removed, and an answer to the question is found on the same paper. The questions suggested were all of such a character that one answer would nearly do for any one. The paper the question was written on had this answer written with invisible ink brought out by a reagent on the blotter, with which it was saturated, and thus another mystery is easily dispelled.

We will now take up a few slate tests, in which the slates are brought or furnished by the spectator or investigator. The tests in which the slates are brought by skeptics and tied and sealed by them, and still writing is obtained upon them, are the ones that are the most convincing and most talked about, and they are offered to the unbeliever as proof absolute of spirit power.

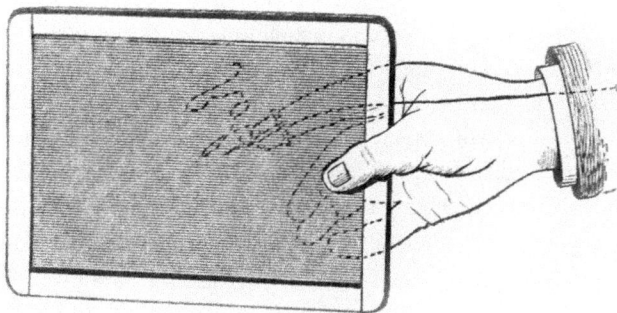

Fig. 6. Writing on the Slate with the Pencil Thimble.

First we will begin with the single slate which has just been handed to the medium, after being thoroughly cleaned by the person bringing it. The skeptic holds one end of the slate in one hand and he medium the opposite end in one of his hands, and both persons clasp their disengaged hands. In a short time the slate is turned over and a few words written in a scrawling style are found. I must acknowledge that when I first witnessed this test it somewhat staggered me, but afterward, on seeing it the second time, I was enabled to fathom its mystery. It is patterned somewhat after the style claimed to have been used by Slade, wherein he used a piece of slate pencil fastened to a thimble, and with apparatus attached to his forefinger of the same hand holding the slate he did the writing. The thimble (Fig. 6) was fastened to an elastic which pulled the thimble out of sight up the sleeve or under the coat when it was done with. But it always required a little scheming and maneuvering both to use and conceal the device and get rid of it, and there was always the fear of being detected with this bit of machinery about the person; so someone of an ingenious turn of mind hit upon another method. There are some slate pencils made he same as lead pencils, that is, a very small piece of slate pencil, about the size of a match, is enclosed in the wood after the manner of lead pencils. A tiny piece of this pencil is placed at the tip of the forefinger and over it is placed a piece of flesh-colored court plaster well fastened to the finger (Fig. 7) and well blended in with aniline dye with the finger, so both are exactly the same color. After everything becomes dry and hard a little hole is made in the court plaster, so as to allow the point of the piece of pencil to come through enough to mark on the slate. The finger thus prepared is what does the writing. The message or name must be written backward, so that when the slate is reversed it will appear in its correct position. To learn to do this quickly, stand in front of a looking-glass with the slate in your hand and watch your writing in the glass as you go along. You do not need to hold the slate underneath the table in this test; hold it in the air with a handkerchief over it, so as to disguise the movement of the finger. The message must necessarily be short, on account of the radius through which the medium's finger can travel.

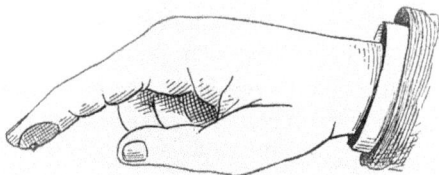

Fig. 7. The Prepared Finger.

We now come to another method of using the single slate. The medium takes the slate and places it on the table and requests the spectator to write a question on a piece of paper. He, the medium, gains knowledge of the contents of the paper in various ways; one is by using a pad of paper which contains underneath the second or third layer of paper a carbon sheet made of wax and lampblack. Whatever is written on the first sheet of paper will be transferred or copied by means of the carbon paper to the sheet underneath it. Another way is by requesting a person to fold the paper and hold it against his head, and, under the pretense of showing the person how to hold it, exchange it for a paper of his own folded in like manner. This exchanged paper is then opened and read by the medium while his hand is below the level of the table top, and while he is holding a conversation with the auditor. After it is read, the paper is again folded and kept in the performer's lap until needed. As he now knows the contents of the paper, he can frame in his mind a suitable answer. He remarks: "I will ask the spirits first to give you a decided answer, through me as an independent trance slate writing medium, whether they will answer your question during this sitting." So the medium takes a pencil in hand and writes on one side of the slate, apparently under spirit control, and then on the other side. The message is read, and it says the conditions are very favorable, and no doubt, if the skeptic will place the utmost confidence in the medium, there will be satisfactory results. After the slate has been shown with both sides covered with writing, it is thoroughly cleaned and placed on the table. The medium now picks up the original paper from his lap and asks the person to give him the paper he is holding. This the medium apparently places under the slate; however, he really holds this one back and introduces the one he has had in his hand, which is the one originally written upon. He has now his own paper in his hand, and the one with the question is under the slate. On the slate being turned over in a short time, it is covered with writing, forming a sensible reply to the question on the paper, which is now opened and read to compare it with the answer. All that remains to be explained is how the writing on the slate appeared there. The false flap is again used, but in a directly opposite manner to which it has been employed heretofore. One side of this flap is covered with a portion of the writing that the medium first wrote under spirit control. Let us say the first half supposed to have been written on the one side of the slate, and which he afterward reads off in connection with that written on the last or second side of the slate. What he really wrote on the first half of the slate was a correct answer to the question, and after he turns the slate over to write on the opposite side he slips the false flap over the answer on the slate. Of course it is what is on this false flap and on the other side of the slate that the spectator really reads, and when the slate is cleaned it is this flap and the opposite side of the slate. The writing, covered by the flap, which is the answer to the question, is never seen or touched until after the flap is allowed to drop into the medium's lap. The slate can be examined; and, of course, no trickery can be found in connection with it. The method described above, in the hands of a calm and cool person, is a convincing one, and never fails to satisfy the most exacting of skeptics.

I wish to remark that, if any person tells you he took two slates of his own to a medium, thoroughly well tied or sealed, and that the slates never left his (the skeptic's) hands, and that there was writing obtained upon the interior surface of the slates under those conditions, he was sadly mistaken, and has failed to keep track of everything that actually took place at the time of the sitting. Suppose two slates tied together are brought to the medium. Both he and the stranger sit at a table. The slates are held under the table, the medium grasping one corner and the skeptic the opposite corner, each with one hand, and the disengaged hands clasped together above the table. After a while the slates are laid upon the table, the string untied, the slates taken apart, but no writing is found. The medium states it must have been because there was no slate pencil between them. So a small piece of pencil is placed between the slates, and again they are tied with the cord by the medium, and he again passes them under the table, both persons holding the slates as before. Presently writing is heard, and, upon the skeptic bringing the slates from under the table and untying the cord himself, he finds one of the slates covered with writing, although but shortly before they were devoid of even a scratch. Here is the explanation: The medium does not pass the slates under the table the first time, but drops them in his lap, with the side on which the string is tied or knotted downward, and really passes a set of his own for the skeptic to hold; he (the medium) supporting his end by pressing against the table with his knee, which leaves his hand disengaged. There is a slate pencil, called the soapstone pencil, which is softer than the ordinary. This is the one used by the medium. He now covers the face of the slate which is uppermost in his lap with writing, doing so very quietly and without any noise. Now, as he brings the slates above the table, he leaves his own in his lap and brings up the skeptic's with the writing side down. The slates are untied and taken apart and shown, devoid of writing upon the inside, which he claims was caused by not having any slate pencil inside. The medium now places the pencil upon the slate which was originally the upper one, and covers this with what was the bottom slate, which is covered with the writing inside on the back or bottom ofslate. This maneuver or action brings the slate on top with the writing upon its inside. Nothing could be more simple and natural. The slates are again tied together, and in doing so the slates are turned over, bringing the slate containing the writing, still upon the inside, at the bottom instead of the top, and the string tied or knotted above the top slate. Of course, when again separated, the writing is found upon the inside of the lower slate. When the slates are passed under the table the second time, the spectator himself is allowed to do this, and the medium, with one of his finger nails, while holding his end of the slate, produces a scratching noise on the slate closely resembling the tracing of a pencil. It is not really necessary to pass the slates under the table the second time, but they can be held above it if preferred.

Now, suppose two slates are brought that are riveted or screwed or sealed at the four corners. How can writing be obtained upon them without disturbing any of the above arrangements? The slates are held under the table in the same manner as in previous tests. To produce the writing upon the slates the medium is provided with a few simple, though effective devices, one of which is a little hard wood tapering wedge, and a piece of thin steel wire, to one end of which is fastened a tiny piece of slate pencil. An old umbrella rib will be found to work admirably, because there is a small clasp at one end and at its other end a small eye. The pencil is made to fit into the end with the clasp. Now take the wooden wedge and push it between the wooden frames of the slates at the sides. The frames and slates will give enough to allow the wire and pencil to be inserted and the writing be accomplished with it, after which the wire is withdrawn, and then also the wooden wedge, and all is done without leaving any trace or mark behind as to how it is all performed. (Fig. 8.)

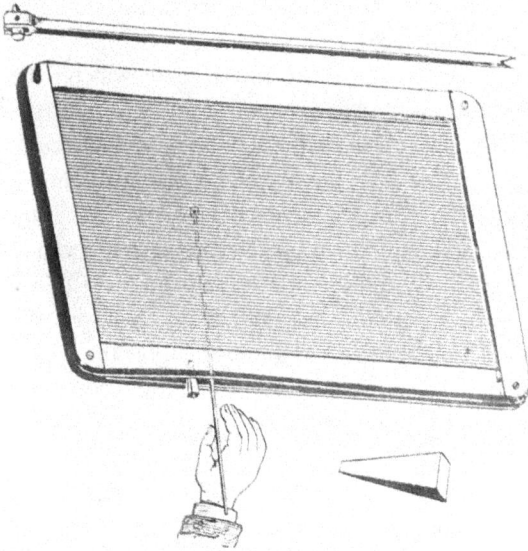

Fig. 8. Wedging Apart the Slates.

A well known conjuror at one time made a remark that he could duplicate any slate writing test he ever witnessed, he having publicly declared, time and time again, the slate writing test to be a fraud. He gave a test in private at his own home and hit upon a rather unique idea. A slate would be cleaned on both sides and a private mark placed on it, and the slate allowed to lie flat on the table, and the magician and the committee sat around it and placed their hands upon the slate. Presently writing was heard, and upon lifting the slate the side underneath was found covered with writing. The table was a kitchen table with the ordinary hanging cloth cover, or table cloth. The table had a double top with room enough between the two to conceal a small boy. There was a neatly made trap in both the table cloth and the top of the table; the cloth being glued around the opening to keep it in place. The trap door opened downwards. The boy concealed in the table opened the trap door and did the necessary writing on the slate, and closed the opening. The idea of having the committee hold their hands on the slate was to prevent the slate from being accidentally moved by the boy when writing. The above idea was improved upon by doing away with the use of the boy and the double top of the table. The trap in the cloth and table top was still used. But the test was done with the lights turned out or down low, and the medium had a confederate sitting at his right hand side. This allowed the medium to take away his right hand, introduce it under the table, open the trap, do the writing, shut the trap, replace his hand, and on the lights being turned up the writing is found. It should be stated that the medium and committee sat around the table with their hands resting on the slate, and each person's hand touching that of his neighbor; so neither could move without the other being aware of the fact, but the medium's right hand neighbor, being one of his confederates, allows him to take his (the medium's) hand away without any one being the wiser.

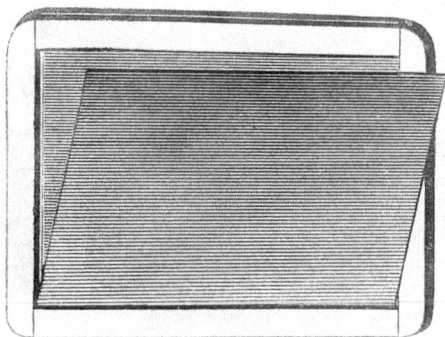

Fig. 9. The Trick Slate.

I will now describe how the writing is obtained upon the interior of two slates sealed together, and all hands placed on them, and without the assistance of a confederate. The table is the same as previously described, that is, it contains the trap. The slates are two single ones hinged together and sealed around the edges in any manner the committee may see fit. One of the slates is a trick slate made in this fashion: The slate part itself is made to work on a pivot or hinge along one of its sides. (Fig. 9.) The side opposite to where both slates are hinged together, by touching a portion of the hinges that hold the two slates together, a catch concealed in the wooden framework is released, which allows the slate part itself to drop down on its own hinge or pivot. So when the slates are placed on the table they are put directly over the trap in the table, and with the hinges of the two slates toward the medium. The medium, as he places the slates over the trap in the table, pushes the hinge releasing the catch, which allows the underneath slate to drop as far as the table. Now, when the trap in the table is opened, the slate opens or drops far enough for the medium to write on that part, also on the slate above it. He closes both the slate and the table, and the slates, upon being unsealed, are found covered with writing. The only thing that remains to be explained is how the medium gets his hand free to do the writing without being

Fig. 10. The Medium Holding the Two Skeptics' Hands.

detected. The lamp or gas jet is close to the medium's right hand, where he can reach it. Now, all the persons are seated around the table with their hands on the slates, and each other's hands or fingers touching one another. The medium takes his right hand away to turn down the light, and his next door neighbor, as soon as the light goes out, feels his (the medium's) hand or finger replaced. At least, so he thinks. What really happens is this: The thumb of the medium's left hand is stretched far enough over to touch the hand or finger of the person sitting on the performer's right hand side. (Fig. 10.) The medium immediately goes to work and produces the writing, and when finished, just as he goes to relight the gas or lamp, he removes the left thumb to create the impression that he has just taken his right hand away again for the light.

Here is a trick I once saw a medium do. He had a number of slates piled on top of the table; he would clean these, one at a time, showing each, and after they had been thoroughly examined, he placed them on the floor. He would then pick them all up together and replace them on the table, and select two of them, put them together, holding them in his hand above his head, would shortly separate them and show one covered with writing. The slates were devoid of all trickery, as was easily proved in allowing them to be thoroughly examined.

Fig. 11. The Slate under the Carpet.

The explanation is as follows: The floor was covered with carpet. In this there was a slit or cut just large enough to pass or draw a slate through. A slate with writing on one side is previously placed under the carpet, with that side down. (Fig. 11.) The slates, as they are cleaned, are laid on the carpet immediately over or near this concealed one, and, on lifting the slates from the floor, this one is also carried with them, and all placed on the table.

Of course, it is this slate and one of the prepared ones that are afterward used. There is little likelihood of any one taking notice of there being one more slate in the pile.

Some mediums use two single slates, and, after cleaning them on both sides, hold one in each hand. They sit a little way from the table and place the right hand, with the slate, under the chair, as if to draw the chair closer to the table. What the medium really accomplishes is an exchange of slates. There is a little shelf, or drawer, under the seat of the chair. On this lies a slate, one side of which is prepared with writing. The medium picks up the slate and leaves behind in its place the one held in his right hand as he moves the chair. This is a method used to a considerable extent and always successfully.

The following is a clever ruse, ofttimes used by mediums to destroy all traces of the use of the false flap when it is employed. It is the test where the flap is used to cover the writing on one slate, and then that slate is covered with another. Now, if the slates are turned over or reversed, the writing is uncovered and the flap remains in the opposite or underneath slate. Now, to get rid of that flap, the medium deliberately presses his knee against that slate, breaking not only the slate, but also the flap contained in it. The broken flap mingles in with the broken slate, and nobody is any the wiser. Nobody for a moment thinks of picking up the pieces to see if there are one or more slates. Of course, when the slates are broken, it is done secretly under the table, and the medium remarks: "The spirit force is so strong it has smashed the slate." A test with a single slate that I once saw done was rather neat in its way, and I think it worth describing. The slate was examined and cleaned on both sides, and placed on a small table covered with a little fancy cloth. On lifting the slate afterward, its underneath side was found with writing on it. The top of the table was no larger than the slate. When the slate was laid on the table, the medium remarked: "To convince you there is no trickery about the table, I will remove the cloth;" which he did, with the slate still on or in it, and then replaced the slate and cloth. Now, on this table top was resting another slate covered with writing on one side, and that side upward, and this covered with the table cloth. When the medium picked up the cloth and the slate, which had just been cleaned, he also carried along the second slate with it, which was under the cloth, and in replacing the cloth he simply reversed the sides, laying the first slate on the table, where it was covered by the cloth, and the second one was thus brought to view. It is astonishing how such barefaced and simple devices will deceive the spectator. It is the boldness and air of conviction of his assertions that carry a medium's test successfully through.

CHAPTER II.

THE DOUBLE SLATE.

We now come to a slate called by the mediums "The double slate." It is, to all appearances, two ordinary slates hinged together at one side and locked with a padlock, the shackle of which passes through a hole in the sides of the frame of each slate. This slate also contains the false flap or slate, but the slate or flap is held firmly in each frame as follows: The inside edges of both ends of each frame of the slates are beveled inward a trifle. One of these ends of each slate frame is also made to slide or pull out about one-quarter of an inch. These are prevented from sliding until wanted by the medium by a catch in the framework, which is connected with a screw in one of the hinges. This screw stands a little higher than the rest, so as to be easily found. The hinges are on the outside of the frame instead of inside. By pressing this screw it undoes the catch, which allows the ends to be moved a trifle. The false flap is just large enough to fill in the space under the bevels of the frame, and if, in the top frame, the catch is released and the end moved, the flap will drop into the bottom slate, where it is held tight and firm by releasing the catch in that frame, moving the end until the flap settles into its place and then sending the end back into its original place again. The writing is placed beforehand on one side of the flap and on one slate, both the written sides face to face, and after the flap has changed slates it presents two slates with written sides.

There is still another double slate used with hinges and padlock. (Fig. 12.)

One of the ends of the wooden frame of one slate is fastened securely to its slate, which is made to slide out completely from the groove in the frame. This allows the insides of both slates to be written upon. After that is done the slate is slid back into its frame. Care should be taken, in sliding the piece back, not to reverse it so as to bring the writing side out. The best way is not to pull the slate completely out, and write upon the inside of the stationary slate, and then reverse the slates, which will bring the inside of the movable slate into view. Write on that and then close the slate.

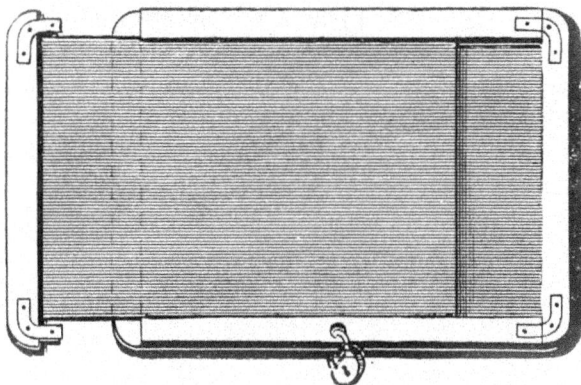

Fig. 12. The Sliding Trick Slates.

I have seen a medium use the double or folding slate and get rid of the false flap in this way: He used a pair of small slates. These he opened out with the flat side towards the audience, and while in his hand, cleaned those two sides away from the table. He now showed the reverse sides and cleaned them likewise. He now closed the slates, but toward him, instead of away from him, holding them close to his body, and as he does so, the false flap, by this movement, slips easily and unperceived beneath his coat or vest.

I once witnessed a test which, for a time, completely nonplussed me, but, after considerable study and experimenting, I solved it.

This is the effect of the test: A person was allowed to bring two slates; he was to wash them himself and securely seal them in the presence of the medium, the medium placing, before the slates were sealed, a piece of chalk between them. The slates were sealed after this fashion: Around the whole length and width of the slates court plaster was stuck, and that was also sealed to the slates with sealing wax, making it an utter impossibility to insert a piece of wire, or like substance, between the slates. Nevertheless, the slates were held under the table and presently removed, unsealed, and writing in a very poor hand found upon the inner surface of one of the slates. It could hardly be called writing, being hardly more than a scrawl.

Now, how can this be accounted for? By one of the simplest devices imaginable. The medium placed the piece of chalk between the slates. This was composed of pulverized chalk, mixed with a little water, glue and iron filings, and allowed to become hard. The medium, while under cover of the table, traced with a magnet below the slate the words found upon the inside, but backward, the same as type is set for printing; if not, the writing on the slate will be in reverse. The chalk, on account of the iron filings it contains, follows the direction of the magnet. (Fig. 13.)

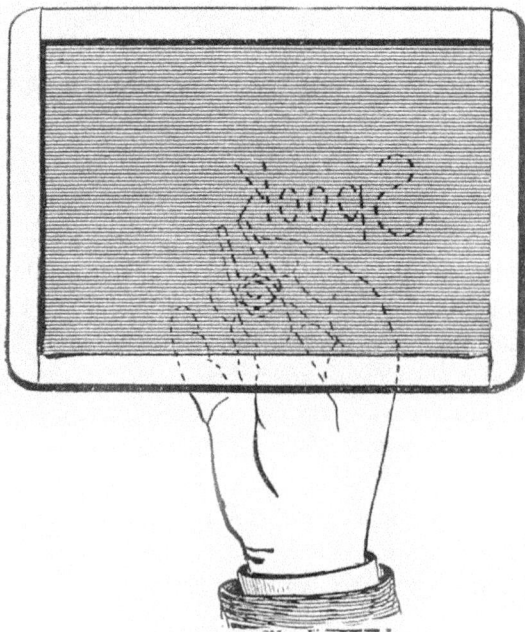

Fig. 13. Magnetic Writing.

We now come to another idea with two slates. Have two slates made with fairly deep wooden frames, deep enough to hold the slate proper and a false flap of slate. One made of silicate book-slate stuff is preferable. Your apparatus consists now of two slates and one false flap. The false flap is made to fit very tightly, so it will not fall out of its own weight. The slates in the frame also fit snugly. The frames are mortised out a little thicker than the slate, say twice as thick. This allows the slate to work backward and forward, from front to back, and *vice versa*. If the slate is well pushed down and the flap placed on it, the flap will not fall out, but if you press the slate on the back forward, it shoves out the flap, and if it is covered with the other or second slate during this operation, it is forced into the second slate, which holds it firm and secure.

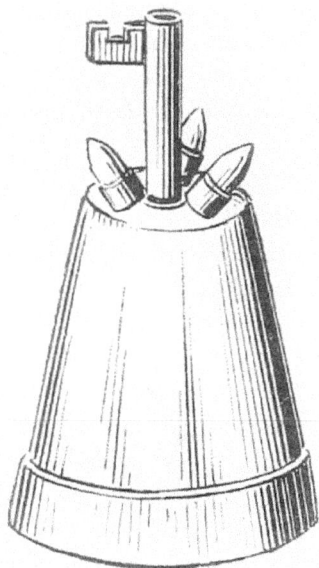

Fig. 14. The Thimble Carrying False Key and Chalks.

Another test, which was supposed to be convincing to skeptics, was one in which a double slate was used; it was hinged and provided with a lock in the wooden frame. The slates were examined, locked, and the key given to the skeptic. The skeptic was allowed to select from a number of pieces of colored chalk the color that he desired the message to be written in. Upon the slates being unlocked and opened, the writing is found in the color selected. While the slates are being examined, the medium seizes a duplicate key which fits the lock. (Fig. 14.) This key has a thimble attached to it which fits the performer's right thumb; also attached lengthwise to the key are several small colored pencils or crayons of different lengths. When the slate has been examined, it is placed under the top of the table and held in position by the thumb of the right hand, which is underneath, and the fingers above the table. During this manipulation the thimble is placed on the thumb, and the performer, with the key attached to it, opens the slate, using his knee to assist or support the slate. One part of the slate opens downward and rests on the knee, which holds it in position, i. e., at an incline, pressing it against the table top. On this part of the slate the writing is now done with the colored crayon selected, which are usually red, blue, green and white. When the color of the crayon is selected the performer turns the thimble around, bringing that color upward. Although not easy to execute, it is, nevertheless, a most surprising and effective test.

The above test was used by a medium very successfully for years in England and France, and was found out recently.

A test I once received was, I thought, quite clever. I was asked to write a question on a piece of paper furnished by myself and place it between two slates without the wooden frames. The medium said I would in a short time receive an answer. He then opened the slates, stating the answer must be there, but none was found. He remarked that perhaps we did not give the spirits time enough. So he replaced the slates together with the paper containing the question between. Again, on taking the slates apart, they were devoid of writing, but, strange to say, the answer in what looked like lead pencil was found on the paper containing the question. When the slates were removed the first time, the medium got a glimpse of the question on the piece of paper and then gave me one slate to examine, and apparently was looking at the other one himself. What he really was doing was this: On the side of the slate toward him he was writing a brief answer to my question with a pencil composed of mutton tallow and lampblack pressed very hard. This pencil was attached to his thumb. He held the slate at the ends with both hands, thumbs behind and fingers in front, the writing being done backward. When the slates were replaced the writing, being black, was not seen against the black slate, and was placed immediately over the paper and the writing transferred to it. This is the reason the slates were used without the wooden frame, because with the frame the two slates would not come close together to press hard enough to transfer the answer.

A test, using a half dozen or so of slates, is as follows: Two slates are cleaned and examined and given to be held together by a skeptic, and the other slates cleaned on both sides and placed on the table. The medium now takes the two slates apart, but no writing is found;

one slate is given to the skeptic and the other is placed on the table by the medium, who picks up another slate and places that with the one held by the unbeliever. After a short time the slates are again removed by the medium and no writing is found. As if in despair, the medium takes one slate away, placing it on the table, picks up another, showing both sides, places it with the one in the spectator's hand, and in a little while the skeptic himself separates the slates and writing is found on one of them.

This method brings in use again the slate with a false flap. This slate is among the others on the table. The two slates first given to the individual to hold are all right when the medium takes one slate away and places it on the table the first time and picks up another slate to place it with the one held by the skeptic. It is the flap slate, and this he places underneath the other slate and asks the skeptic to hold them. When the medium again separates the slates he turns them over, bringing the slate with the writing uppermost and also allowing the flap to fall into the lower slate, which is now taken away to be replaced by another taken from the table. Care is taken not to show the underneath side of the upper slate during this transaction. The slates the skeptic now holds are devoid of trickery, and when exposed with the writing on will cause wonderment.

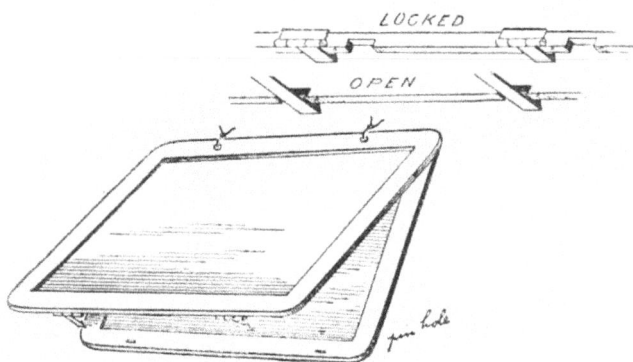

Fig. 15. Slate with False Hinges.

There is still another style of slate made, and used to good advantage. It is two slates hinged together, making a double slate. It has also two holes in the frame opposite to the hinges, through which tape or cord can be run and tied and sealed to the slates. (Fig. 15.) The secret of getting the writing upon the inside lies in the fact that at least one-half of each hinge is screwed to the slate; the other half is made fast to a little projecting piece in which there is a slight notch. These projections enter corresponding holes in the other slate, in which is concealed a spring bolt which engages these catches of the hinge. This bolt is shoved back to release the catches by means of a pin pushed through a hole in the end of the frame.

CHAPTER III.

MISCELLANEOUS SLATE TESTS.

At a public test or séance given by a medium I saw the following clever trick performed: A slate, clean on both sides, to all appearances, and, of course, devoid of writing, was given to a spectator to hold above his head. The medium then loaded a pistol, putting in, instead of a bullet, a piece of chalk, which he rammed well in. He then took careful aim at the slate, fired away, and the slate was covered with writing from the chalk that was placed in the pistol. The medium, beforehand, allows any one in the audience to choose from a plate containing different colored chalks the colors they desire. The chalk is all right, and is actually placed in the pistol and crushed to a powder by the ramrod. The slate has been written on one side with glycerine. This side of the slate is supposed to be cleaned, so as to keep clear of the glycerine, in order that the invisible writing may not be disturbed. It is this prepared side that faces the medium when he fires the pistol. The powdered chalk adheres to the glycerine, and thus we make clear another slate miracle.

A clever trick employed to deceive me on one occasion was as follows: I was handed a slate and a damp sponge, with a request to cleanse the slate. I did so, and handed it back to the medium, who held it in plain view in one hand. In a short time the slate was given back to me with writing on it that could not be produced by any of the methods I was already acquainted with. I witnessed this test a second time, and it was only by accident that I discovered it, and all through the breaking of a string, to which the device employed was attached. The apparatus was a strip of narrow wood, nearly the length of the slate. Glued on it were raised letters of cork (felt would do also). These letters were in reverse, and were well rubbed with soft chalk. This strip of wood was attached to a cord running up the left sleeve, across the back, and down the right arm-hole, and thence under the vest and the end fastened to a button. The length of the string allowed the wood to hang behind the slate when held in the left hand. To keep the wood up in the sleeve until wanted, there was a loop on the string far enough up to suit the purpose. This loop was slipped over the button, where it could be easily detached with the right hand. The sponge was soaked in water containing alum, which makes the chalk adhere better to the slate. When the slate was handed to the medium, he held it downward in his left hand, and allowed the strip of wood to slip down behind it, when it was pressed firmly against the surface of the slate, and then pulled up into the sleeve again out of sight. This same idea has been utilized in using a blotter, the same as is used for ink, to dry the slate with. The blotter has the writing done on it with chalk, thus doing away with the strip of wood.

Take a slate and cover it with writing on one side. Cover this writing with a piece of slate-colored silk, held in the corners lightly with wax. At one end of this silk have a few minute hooks. The slate is now cleaned on both sides, and, placing the slate on the floor, the piece of silk is allowed to attach itself by means of the hooks to the medium's pants, or dress, as the case may be, thus leaving the slate devoid of trickery. It is hardly necessary to remark that the slate is placed on the floor written-side downward.

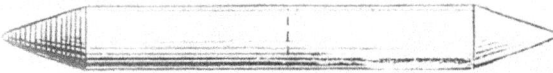

Fig. 16. The Caustic Trick Pencil.

A friend of mine told me of a medium he once went to see, who gave him a most remarkable test. He brought his own slate, and, as he afterward said, there could have been no trick about it. The medium took the slate for a moment, and with a pencil covered the slate with writing on both sides, just to see, so he said, if it would be good enough for the test. He then cleaned off the slate on both sides and gave it back to my friend, requesting him to hold it close against his breast, and then in a short time remove it, and, when he did so, he was thunderstruck to find writing on it on the side nearest to him. This struck me as being a most astounding proof of spirit writing. I had a meeting with the medium, who gave me the same test. It seemed strange to me that he should want my slate to write on and wash it off again, for the same reason as he gave my friend, and that was to see "if it was good enough for the spirits to work with." I received a message on the slate, after it was washed, and saw that there was none on there after it was cleaned and handed to me. I went home puzzled, and experimented to no avail. I had another sitting with the medium, but he did not give me the same test; so I returned home again and tried to fathom the mystery, and was eventually successful. The trick was mainly in the pencil. It was pointed at both ends. (Fig. 16.) One end was a genuine slate pencil, the other end was a silver nitrate, or caustic pencil. In writing on the slate he wrote the lines quite a little distance apart with the slate pencil; in between these lines he wrote with the caustic pencil, the writing of which was invisible. The sponge the slate was cleaned with, was dipped in salt water. That part of the slate containing the writing done with the silver nitrate was just lightly tapped with the sponge, the rest of the slate was thoroughly cleaned. The salt water, when the slate becomes dry, brings out the silver nitrate white like a slate pencil mark. I consider this trick as ingenious and clever a one as it has been my good fortune to witness, and one that caused me much mental effort to solve.

Here is another test. A slate just cleaned and marked is placed under the table on the floor. The medium and the skeptic grasp each other's hands across the table. In a few seconds the slate is taken up from the floor and is found with writing on it. The solution of this, like all the rest of the slate phenomena, rests in simplicity and boldness. The medium wears slippers or low-cut shoes, that he can slip his foot out of easily. His stocking on his right foot is cut away so as to leave the toes bare. Now, attached to his great toe is a bit of pencil, and with this the writing is done. (Fig. 17.) Sometimes the test is varied. Five or six pieces of chalk of different colors are on the table, and the investigator is allowed to select one, place it on the slate. In this case the chalk is held between the great and adjoining toe, and the writing is thus produced. It is surprising to see, with a little practice, what you can educate the foot to do. I myself can easily pick a pin off the floor and write quite well. Sometimes, by way of variation,

Fig. 17. Writing with the Toes.

instead of the medium or investigator lifting the slate from the floor, it is seen to mysteriously make its appearance above the edge of the table, being lifted there by means of the toes of the medium's foot. Another method used is that of scratching the writing on the slate with any metal instrument and then wash the slate on both sides, being careful not to show the scratched side until it is wet from the washing. In this condition a casual glance will reveal nothing, but as soon as the slate becomes dry the writing or scratching appears. Writing has also been made to appear on a slate on the table while the medium and investigator sit with both hands clasped across the table. The medium accomplished this by the simple means of a pencil concealed in his mouth. At the proper moment he holds it between his teeth, leans his head over and writes on the slate. Of course this is all done in the dark, and the writing is not very good, but it answers the purpose, and that is all that is necessary.

Here is still another test. A person writes a question on the slate and places it, written side down, on the table. All this when the medium is not looking. The medium takes his seat at the table, places one hand on the slate (so does the skeptic, the other hand on the medium's forehead). With the disengaged hand the medium now proceeds to write on the upper surface of the slate. When he has finished, the communication is read, and it is found to be a correct answer to the question on the opposite side of the slate. To perform this seeming impossibility the medium has to employ a table containing a trap smaller than the frame of the slate. When the slate is placed on the table, the medium shifts it over this trap. The trap is then opened, and by means of mirrors, 3, 4, 5, placed at angles of 45 degrees in the body of the table, the writing is reflected to the very place where the medium is sitting, and the image is reversed to normal by the third mirror, and it is easy then to give an answer to it. (Fig. 18.)

Fig. 18. Reading the Questions by Means of Mirrors.

The following is how writing can be made to appear on a slate on which a person has placed his initials in one corner of it, which is then placed with that side downward on the table, and shortly afterward, on turning it over, it is found completely covered with writing, and the signature of the visitor proves there has been no exchange of the slate. The secret of obtaining this effect is both a unique and quite original method.

The writing is already on the slate and is hidden from view by the false flap, which has a corner missing from it. This missing corner is where the clever idea comes in. After the medium cleans both sides of the slate, he says: "I will just draw a chalk mark down in this corner of the slate wherein the gentleman is to place his signature." He really draws the chalk mark on the slate proper, but close to the edge of the missing corner of the flap, thus disguising the joint, and after the flap is dropped out of the slate of course this mark and signature still remains. (Fig. 19.)

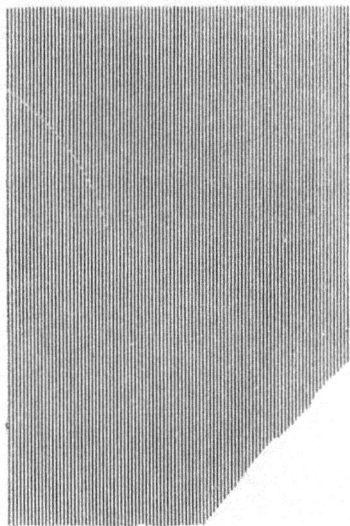

Fig. 19. The Interrupted Flap.

Here is still another. The medium cleans a slate on both sides and hands it to a skeptic to place his mark on it. It is then placed on the table, face downward, and in a short time, on being turned over, it is found with a spirit message on it. This is performed as follows: Let the message be written on the slate and then sponged out with alcohol, and when the slate dries, the writing will be as plain as ever.

Here is another slate writing secret. Dissolve in hydrochloric acid some small pieces of pure zinc, about one-half ounce to an ounce of acid. With this solution write upon the slate with a quill or a small camel's hair brush the desired communication. When dry it closely resembles writing done with a slate pencil. When the time arrives for the test, wash the slate, and it appears to be perfectly clean; allow any one to examine it and hold it until it becomes dry, but with the prepared side down. On the slate being turned over it is found to be covered with writing while in the spectator's hand.

Here is still another idea. The medium has a number of slates in his arms, say four. He hands the investigator the top one to clean. When he has done so, the medium receives it back and places it at the bottom of the pile of slates and hands him another again from the top to be cleaned, and repeats this operation until all four slates have been cleaned. He now takes two of the slates, places them together, and, on removing them again, writing is found on one of them. Here is the method of procedure: Prepare your communication on one of the slates, and let it be the bottom of the pile, with the writing side down. Have your visitor seated, stand by his side just a trifle behind him, hand him the top slate to clean; after he has done so, hand him the second one and receive the first one back, placing it at the bottom of all the slates, and repeat until the third slate. While this one is being cleaned, slip the fourth, now the top slate, to the bottom again. When the third slate is received, place it on the bottom and hand the fourth, really the first one over again; it is, of course, the top one and dry by this time, and the investigator is none the wiser. Of course, the two slates placed together afterward are the one prepared with writing and one of the blank ones. Instead of slipping the top slate to the bottom, sometimes another dodge is used. The medium simply turns the three slates over by a twist of the hand. This brings the prepared slate at the bottom and the last slate cleaned at the top, and he says he will clean this one, thus saving time; really, however, to disguise the fact that it is still wet from the last cleaning. He says, however, to the visitor, "You can clean it also, if you desire."

CHAPTER IV.

MIND READING AND KINDRED PHENOMENA.

Having now described the principal slate tricks which mediums use to entangle the unwary for their own ends, we come to other tricks which are used from time to time to impress the credulous with the idea that the medium is imbued with supernatural power and can perform what are, in effect, miracles. These tricks are legion, and they vary from clumsy attempts at mystification to the use of elaborate pieces of magical apparatus which call for rare mechanical genius in their design and construction. The present chapter will deal more particularly with what might be termed mind reading tricks and the reading of concealed writing. Of these tricks one of the most perplexing is that of reading sealed communications, or answering questions placed in an envelope which is well sealed.

If I were to tell you that I could read whatever was written on a card inclosed in an envelope, and that envelope not only well sealed, but also stitched or sewn through with a thread and needle or machine, and the thread sealed to the envelope also, without removing the seal, stitches, etc., you would hardly credit the assertion. It is nevertheless true, and is easily and readily accomplished by very simple means.

Prepare a sponge with alcohol. With this you rub or brush the envelope, which immediately becomes transparent as glass, thus enabling you to see through it and read what is written on the card. It takes but a few seconds for the alcohol to evaporate and leave the envelope in the same condition as before, without leaving a trace as to what or how it has done. This test was used most successfully for years by a celebrated Philadelphia medium.

We now come to a test often employed. A card is given by the medium to a skeptic with the request to write a question on it. The medium now holds the card in his hand against his forehead. Presently he hands the card back to the spectator, and on it, in writing, is found an answer to the question. The medium accomplishes the above feat by means of a little apparatus which is easily attached to the tip of the thumb. Part of it goes under the thumb nail and the lower part has a small needle point which embeds itself in the flesh. In the center of this little apparatus is a tiny piece of lead pencil. With this clever bit of mechanism the medium does the writing with the thumb of the hand holding the card. (Fig. 20.)

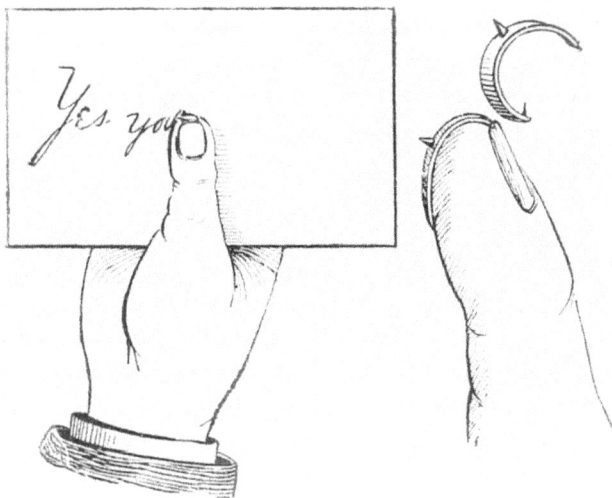

Fig. 20. The Thumb Pencil Carrier.

Four or five persons are seated around a table. They are given paper and pencil and requested to write questions, then fold their papers up and place them in their pockets. The medium will give them replies to their questions; in fact, can tell them the full text of the questions they asked, and, what is more mysterious, he has been out of the room all the time the writing has been going on. To produce this effect, you are provided with a table containing a hollow leg. Now, spread a piece of thin white silk on top of table, then on the top of that a piece of carbon, or duplicating paper, or cloth. Now, over all, a thin table cover, fastened around the edges, so it cannot be raised up and looked under by the inquisitive.

To the white piece of silk is fastened a string leading down the hollow leg, through a hole in the flooring, to the cellar or room below. Whatever writing is placed on the papers is transferred by the carbon paper to the silk below it. The medium pulls the string, down comes the silk. One corner of the silk has a mark corresponding with a certain corner of the table, and by this method not only does the medium know what is written, but who wrote it, as he has simply to see the position the writing occupies on the silk, and it will have been done by the party occupying the same position at the table. Another way is by using a pad of soft paper and hard pencils, and, after the writing, remove the pads. It will be found that the hard pencil has caused an imprint, or indenture, of the writing on the page below, not readily seen by a casual glance, but easily seen by the skilled eye of the medium.

A test sometimes offered is as follows: A card is offered to a person to write a request. It is then placed in an envelope and sealed by the medium and placed on the table sealed side up. The medium now takes a pencil and slate and writes something on it. It is given to the skeptic who wrote the question, and it is found to be an answer to his query. The medium now opens the envelope by tearing it at one end, and takes out the card containing the question and hands it to the spectator. This is another humbug, and is accomplished by exceedingly simple but bold means. It will be observed that the medium places the card in the envelope, also takes it out. The skeptic never sees it. This is the secret: The envelope, on its face, has a slit cut in it a little lower down than the opening on the other side of the envelope. This side, the face of the envelope, is never shown. The card, in being placed in the envelope, is deliberately pushed through the slit in the envelope into the medium's hand and palmed by him and read. Of course, it is an easy matter to write some kind of a sensible answer when the question is known. The card is inserted in the envelope in the same manner as it is taken out.

Another trick is to have an answer appear written upon the inside of the body of the envelope in which is enclosed the question. The envelope is closed and sealed with sealing wax. This is accomplished without disturbing the seal. In the ordinary manufacture of an envelope, three of the flaps are stuck together with adhesive gum of far less strength than the fourth flap, which is to be moistened and closed by the user. It is generally an easy matter to insert the blade of a penknife behind the bottom flap, that is, between it and one of the end flaps, and separate them a trifle. Then, if you insert into this a wooden skewer, or hard, round-pointed stick, like a pencil, in fact, a lead pencil will do, but look out it does not leave marks behind; and by pushing this along, and giving it a rolling motion, you will separate the flaps up as far as the seal, and, if done carefully, without tearing or mutilating the envelope. Now, on a slip of paper write the answer or suitable message, but in reverse or backward writing, as the words would appear in a looking-glass, with a carbon or copying pencil. Pass this slip through the opening in the envelope, shake it into the desired position, now rub the envelope over this spot until you think the envelope has taken the impression. Then remove the slip of paper by the same way it came in, moisten and gum the opening, and the trick is done. In rubbing the envelope, it is a good plan to place a piece of paper over it to keep the envelope clean of marks, which would be liable to appear from damp or moist fingers during the rubbing.

The following is from the experiments of a German scientist. He discovered, by the use of an embryoscope, or egg-glass, that the shells of eggs were of very unequal thickness.

It occurred to him to make experiments in order to ascertain how many leaves of ordinary letter or official paper must be laid above and below a written leaf, in order to make it illegible to a highly sensitive eye in the direct sunlight. He found that after he had rested his eye in a dark room for ten or fifteen minutes, he could read a piece of writing over the mirror of the embryoscope that had been covered with eight layers of paper. He called in other observers to confirm this. The letters, however, that could be thus deciphered were written in dark ink on one side of the paper only. If four written sides were folded together, and especially if there had been crossing, it was hard to make out the drift of the writing; and there are some kinds of writing which, when folded thrice or twice, admit too little light for the purpose of decipherment.

In this way, possibly, many of the performances of "clairvoyants" may be explained. By means of the egg-glass it is, as a rule, easier to make out the contents of a letter or telegram without the slightest tampering with the envelope than it is to detect the movements of the embryo in the egg.

Suppose the writer of a billet, the contents of which are known only to himself, lets it out of his hands and loses sight of it for five minutes, it may be carried either in the direct sunlight, or into electric or magnesium light, and be read by the aid of the egg-glass. The placing of a piece of cartridge paper in the envelope, or the coloring of it black, is a means of defense at hand. In their present form, telegrams cannot be protected from perusal, unless delivered at once into the hands of the addressees.

A few tests employed by mind readers and clairvoyants, so called from their presumed ability to read other people's minds, will, I think, prove interesting. Let us suppose the performer, as a means of proving his ability to cause his subject to read his mind from a distance, or by mental telegraphy, execute the following feat. His subject, let us say his wife, is at home. The professor is in a public place, a store, or banking house, etc. He requests some one to write a question; he hands this person a fountain pen and a pad of paper. After the person has done so, he is requested to fold the communication up, place it in an envelope and seal it, and then put it in his pocket. He is now asked to write a letter or note to the professor's assistant, asking her to inform him what it was that he had asked on the paper inclosed in the envelope in his pocket. This note, and the pen also, for fear the lady has no writing utensils, is carried by the gentleman himself to the lady. She reads the request, and, turning the paper over, she writes the answer correctly on the other side. Sometimes, instead of the gentleman himself going with the note, a messenger boy is sent with it and the answer brought back by him. In either case the paper and pen are sent along. The pen is an ordinary fountain pen, and it is by means of it that the lady receives the desired information of what has been written. First the professor has to know what has been written. He simply says to the gentleman: "You must allow me to read the question; for, if I do not see it, how can my assistant see it, for it is through me she is enabled to know? What I see I convey to her by mental telegraphy, and thus convey the communication." After the professor sees the communication he goes to a desk and gets an envelope, or takes one out of his pocket, and gives it to the gentleman to place his question in and seal it. While this is being done he stealthily writes on a piece of fine, thin paper an exact copy of the question. This he makes into a little pellet and places it in the little cap or end that is made to cover the point of the pen for protection. Of course it is now easy to see the method by which the question is made known to the assistant. She has simply to remove the pellet of paper, unfold it and read it. Sometimes a pad of paper is used that has cunningly concealed between two of its leaves, near the top, a piece of carbon duplicating paper. These two sheets are pasted around the edges so as to appear as one, and when the person writes a question it is duplicated on the sheet of paper following the one wherein is concealed the carbon paper. The professor has simply to tear out this sheet and inclose it in the cap of the fountain pen. The name of Foster is almost invariably coupled with any test wherein there is reading of sealed letters, pellets, etc., just the same as Slade's is connected with the slate writing tests.

Foster was an inveterate smoker, anywhere and everywhere, especially at his séance, and it was all for a purpose. The visitor who desired a sitting with Foster was asked to write a few questions on small pieces of paper, fold them up separately, and press them into small balls or pellets. Foster would pick one of these up and hold it to his head, as if to try and penetrate it. Apparently failing to do so, he would place it back on the table. This he would repeat with others. Finally, he hands one of them to the visitor, after holding it against his forehead, requesting him to hold it himself. Foster then took a pencil and paper, and scribbled something on it, and then bared one of his arms, and showed it devoid of any preparation. He then rubbed this arm with his hand, and, on removing it, a name was seen. On reading what Foster scribbled on the paper, the visitor finds an answer to one of his questions, and the name in blood red on Foster's arm is found to be the name of a person addressed by the visitor in the note. Foster had a pellet of paper of his own concealed between his finger tips, and, at some convenient moment, instead of placing back on the table one of the pellets he has just taken up, he substitutes one of his own, keeping the bona fide one in his hand, which he lowers into his lap and unfolds. Holding it in the palm of his hand, he strikes a match and lights his cigar, and while doing so he is deliberately reading the note, which he afterward crumples into a ball and conceals in his hand. He now takes up another pellet and tries to see through it by holding it to his forehead. He, however, fails, and gives it to the visitor to hold, really exchanging it for the one he has just read. He now has his own and the visitor has his. He now allows his hands to lie carelessly in his lap, and, while conversing with the visitor, he pushes one of his coat sleeves up a short distance, and, with a sharp-pointed stick, writes the desired name on his arm, pressing down hard. In a second or two he writes the answer to the visitor's question, minus the name he has just placed on his arm. He now shows his arm bare, and rubs the spot where he has written, with his fingers slightly moistened, whereupon the name appears in bright pink writing. If it is desired to make it disappear, hold the hand above the head a few seconds. To make it appear again, rub once more with the fingers.

Here is another trick which apparently calls for mind reading. The performer's assistant is sent out of the room. Now, a sum of figures in addition is placed on the slate by a spectator. When he has concluded, the performer takes the chalk and draws a line under the numbers, turns the slate downward on a table, so nothing can be seen, places chalk on the slate, and retires into a corner of the room. His assistant is now called into the room, steps up to the table and seizes the chalk and marks down the correct answer to the sum of figures which is on the other side. Like all the tricks that appear the most incomprehensible, this is one of the most simple. The performer stands watching the person as he places down the numbers on the slate, he mentally adds them, and, with his hands behind his back or under his coat-tails, with a lead pencil in one hand, he writes on a piece of chalk held in the other hand the correct answer. It is needless to say that it is this piece of chalk he places on the slate, and not the one used. The chalk is scraped or filed flat a trifle lengthwise. This is to keep it from rolling on the slate, thus avoiding accidental exposure of the writing on it, and also give it a flat surface to write on.

Here is an effect I produced as a stage illusion some years ago, somewhat resembling a spiritualistic effect. Hanging up against the scene, at the rear of the stage, was a large blackboard. On this black-board writing appeared gradually, done in chalk, as though some un-seen hand were actually at work. The blackboard was really nothing but fine wire slate-colored netting. There was a large hole cut in the scene immediately behind the blackboard. This hole was completely boxed in by curtains or woodwork, so as to make it as dark as night. A man was in this space, and he was dressed in a complete suit of black; also a black mask and gloves. He was provided with a pot of white paint, composed of whiting, water and glue, and a brush. Now, the man can see through this netting, but the spectators are unable to see him behind this screen of netting. With the brush and paint he traces on the wire netting whatever is desired. The paint comes through the meshes of the netting, and, adhering to it, makes a very good imitation of a chalk mark. It should be remembered the person doing the writing does so backward; so it will be in correct position when seen by the audience.

Fig. 21. The Board Facing the Audience.

The following is somewhat in the same line, and is called the "Educated Fly." When the curtain rises a large mirror, in a gilt frame, is seen resting against an easel. (Fig. 21.) The magician takes the mirror in its frame from the easel and rests it on the floor, showing both sides to the audience. He also removes the glass from the frame, and rests the glass against the easel while he exhibits the frame to the audience. The frame has a solid wooden back. The mirror is about four and a half feet wide and three feet high, and after it has been inspected, the magician replaces it in the frame. He now takes a piece of soap and marks the glass off into twenty-eight even squares, which he numbers from one to twenty-six, and letters from A to Z; one of the remaining squares is zero, and the other is left, as the prestidigitateur says, for a starting point. He now takes a large fly from the table and places it on a little shelf which projects from the empty square. He then asks that a letter or number be called. As soon as this is done, the fly is seen to travel across the mirror and stop at the desired square. This is repeated time and time again, the fly every time returning to the starting point.

Fig. 22. The Mystery Explained.

The reason for having the mirror separate from its frame, and exhibiting it separately, is this: It will be remembered that the mirror is rested against the easel as the frame is shown, and that this frame has a wooden back. In addition to the wooden back, it has a cloth back, which is firmly fastened to the frame, and then comes the wooden back. This back is hinged to the frame at the bottom. Now, when the frame is placed on the easel and the mirror rested on the floor, the space behind the easel from the floor up is concealed by the mirror, and this gives an opportunity for a boy to get through a trap in the floor and pull down the back of the frame, to make a shelf on which he sits. (Fig. 22.) Of course, the cloth back is still in the frame; so the boy cannot be seen. The mirror is taken up and replaced in the frame; then it is marked off into squares, as already mentioned. The black cloth is previously marked off into squares which exactly duplicate those which have been made on the face of the mirror. The fly is made of cork, with an iron core which is set flat against the glass.

The boy behind the mirror is provided with a strong electro-magnet attached to a wire running down the leg of the easel and under the stage, where it is connected to a powerful battery. He brings up the magnet and several feet of wire with him while the mirror is resting on the stage. When the boy hears the numbers called, he applies his magnet to the corner where the fly is resting on the little shelf, and the magnetic attraction, working through the glass, draws it successively over the squares until it comes to the desired spot, which the boy can see on his chart; and, of course, the proper letter or figure is indicated where the fly stops.

The most sphinx-like problem ever presented to the public for solution was the second-sight mystery. There have been many exposés of "mental magic," and some of the best of them are described in "Magic: Stage Illusions and Scientific Diversions, Including Trick Photography."

We have now to concern ourselves with "mental magic" where the results are obtained by clever tricks. There have appeared, from time to time, before the public, individuals who generally work in couples, termed "operators" and "subjects," who have given performances which were termed mental wonders, silent second-sight, etc.

The operator invariably tries to impose on the public with the idea that he possesses some mysterious power over the "subject" by which he is enabled to communicate information to her by his will power over her mind, without a word being spoken. There are, of course, various methods of performing this trick, as by a code of predetermined signals in which sentences like the following are used: "Say the number. Well? Speak out. Say what it is." But these methods are not comparable with the mechanical means which we are about to describe.

The "operator," after informing the audience of the wonderful powers of divination which the subject possesses, introduces the "subject," who is invariably a lady. She is seated on a chair near the front of the stage, in plain view of the audience. Her eyes are heavily bandaged, so she cannot see. A committee is invited to go upon the stage to see that the lady has had her eyes properly blindfolded, and also, ostensibly, to help the operator. A large blackboard is placed at one side of the stage, behind the lady. One of the committee is requested to step to this blackboard and write on it, with chalk, some figures, usually up to four or more decimal places; and after he has done so

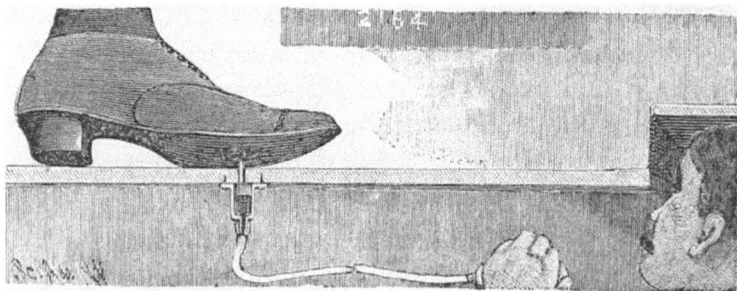

Fig. 23. The Foot Telegraph.

he resumes his seat. The lady immediately appears to add up the number mentally, calling out the numbers and giving the results of the addition. Each member of the committee is invited to step to the blackboard and touch a figure. No sooner has he done so than the lady calls out the number. Other tests of a similar nature are given, such as the extraction of square and cube root, etc. They all prove that the lady has a thorough knowledge of the numbers on the blackboard and the relative position which they occupy. It is, of course, proved beyond a doubt that the lady cannot see the blackboard. The question then arises, How does she obtain the information? There are two methods of performing this trick. In either case her information is obtained from a confederate, who is generally concealed under the stage, who has the blackboard in sight, and who transmits to the lady the desired information.

In one method the lady has a hole, one and a half inches in diameter, cut out of the sole of one of her slippers. (Fig. 23.) She places this foot over a hole in the stage, through which a small piston is

Fig. 24. The Speaking Tube.

worked pneumatically by the assistant. The piston is connected with a rubber tube, which runs to where the assistant is concealed. The assistant looks at the blackboard and manipulates the bulb, thus caus-ing the piston rod to strike the sole of the foot, giving signals which can be readily understood by the subject. Robert Heller used a system somewhat similar, only an electro-magnet was used instead of the pneumatic piston.

Another and bolder method of conveying information is the speaking tube. In this case a Vienna bent-wood chair is used. The chair is specially prepared for the trick. One leg of the chair is hollow, and the air passage is continued to the very top. The lady usually has a long braid of hair hanging down her back, and, if not blessed by nature with this hirsute adornment, she wears a wig. In either case, concealed in the hair is a rubber tube, one end being close to the ear and the other hanging down with the braid, so that when the lady is seated on the chair the operator can easily connect it with the tube in the chair. (Fig. 24.)

Fig. 25. The Head Telegraph.

Fig. 26. The Signaling Instrument.

There is still a third method, which is so absurdly simple that it deceives even a very knowing committee. The committee places a chair on any part of the stage they may see fit, and the subject seats herself and is blindfolded as before. A thread runs from the side of the subject through a small ring attached to a chandelier overhead. (Fig. 25.) One end of this thread is held by an assistant and the other end is fastened to a hammer working on a pivot secured to a metal plate concealed in the hair of the lady, her hair being dressed high. When she walks on the stage, the assistant pulls in the slack of the thread, and when she is seated on the chair, the assistant pulls the thread taut, so that he is able to communicate signals to her by a very slight motion of the thread, which causes the hammer to work on the plate, which is resting very close to the skull, so that the signals are easily felt at every stroke of the hammer. (Fig. 26.) Predetermined signals may be used, or the regular Morse alphabet, as in telegraphing. There are a number of other ways of convey conveying information, but the three methods we have described are perhaps the best.

CHAPTER V.

TABLE LIFTING AND SPIRIT RAPPING.

So much has been heard about table tipping and floating tables, it will, I think, prove interesting to explain a few of the clever devices employed to produce the above phenomena. Small, light tables are lifted by the mere "laying on of hands." The arms are raised in the air and the table is seen to cling to the hands and follow every motion. This is accomplished by a pin driven well into the table, and a ring with a slot in it (Fig. 27) worn on one of the medium's fingers. The body of the pin easily enters the slot in the ring, but the head of the pin, being larger, prevents the table from falling away from the hand. After the table has been floated successfully, an extra strong upward

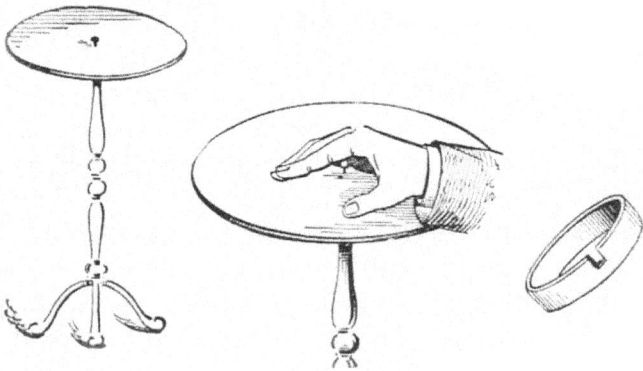

Fig. 27. Table Lifting Trick.

pressure of the hand pulls the pin out, and the table can be examined. Another test on somewhat similar lines is the lifting of a bowl of water by immersing the hand in the basin of water. In this case a pin is fastened firmly into a leather or rubber sucker, and the finger ring again does the work. (Fig. 28.) This can also be used to lift anything that is not of a porous nature. A table with a well polished top can be easily lifted. In lifting large tables the medium is assisted by a confederate among the assembled guests. It is his duty to get as near opposite the medium as possible. The medium and the confederate

Fig. 28. The Sucker.

have fastened to their wrists, by means of a leather cuff and straps, a bent hook. (Fig. 29.) Their hands rest on top and the hooks under the table. By this means it is a simple task to raise the table. Sometimes the above device is varied; instead of hooks fastened to their wrists they use hooks from under their vests, hanging by a loop from their necks. (Fig. 30.) I have seen a square table lifted without the use of either of the above devices. The medium and his confederate simply got the linen cuffs of their right hands well under the corner of the table, and with their hands on top they found no difficulty in raising the table by this improvised means.

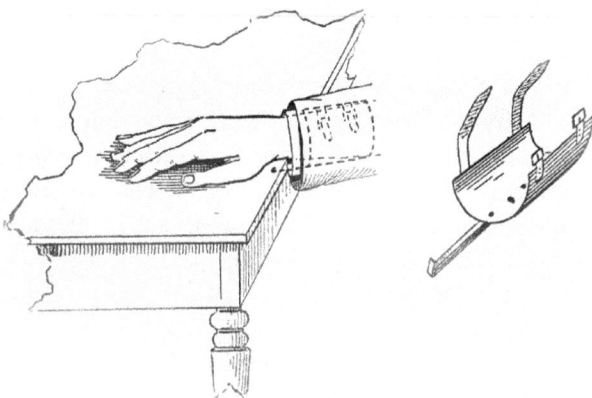

Fig. 29. The Leather Cuff and Hook.

Although spiritualists claim they have, and can, make pianos float in the air, I have never seen it accomplished, and I could never get a medium who was able to produce the effect, and I sincerely doubt if any one can honestly and truthfully acknowledge they have witnessed it.

I saw a small, round table once floated in the air without the medium touching it. It was accomplished by means of two threads running across the room and worked by two confederates. The threads were on the floor and lifted up and allowed to catch under the table.

I have also seen a letter raised from a table and float in the air into the medium's hand. This was done also with a thread, one end fastened in the wall above the table the letter rested on, the other near the medium. The letter is not sealed. This allows the thread to go between the flap and letter, or envelope, and when the medium pulled the thread taut, it made an incline for the envelope to travel on, right up to the outstretched hand.

Fig. 30. The Loop and Hook for Table Raising.

Years ago Robert-Houdin, the celebrated French conjurer, produced, at his pretty little theater in Paris, an illusion which, for startling effects, has not since that time been excelled; and the means which he employed for operating the stage machinery have been employed in many stage tricks of more recent date. The stage is set to represent a drawing-room, and, in stage parlance, would be called a "box set." There are side scenes, as well as a "drop" or back piece. In the center of the room is a large door, and a grand piano rests against one of the side scenes, a small table being placed near the door. When the illusion is to be performed, a lady enters carrying a bouquet, which she leaves on the table and advances to the piano. (See Frontispiece.) She seats herself, opens the cover of the piano and plays a short piece; then, closing down the cover, remarks that she does not feel in the humor to play. She extends her hand toward the bouquet on the table, which mysteriously rises and falls through the air into her hand; and, at the same time, she is seen to rise upward in the air still seated upon the piano stool. When she reaches a point midway between the ceiling and the floor she glides toward the opposite sides of the room, and the piano, which seems as if it will not be outdone, rises also and follows her through the air. This is usually received with great applause by the audience, and the curtain falls. The explanation of the phenomena is the following (Fig. 31): In the first place, the piano case is cleverly made out of *papier maché*, and is really a mere shell containing no keyboard or action. The back of the piano is open; immediately behind it, in the side scene, is a trap, and at the back of this scene is a real piano mounted on a truck, so that it can be easily moved backward and forward. Our engraving shows both the piano and the trap. When the real piano is run into the *papier maché* case the keyboard is in its normal position, so that the lady can play upon it. When the lady finishes playing she closes the lid of the false piano. As soon as this is done an assistant behind the scene moves the piano back, thus leaving the empty shell, and the trap in the scene is closed. The false piano is, of course, very light, and to it are fastened fine wires, which are invisible at a short distance; one is secured to each corner. These wires run up over pulleys on a truck overhead, which can be run backward and forward immediately over the scene. Each wire is terminated by a bag of sand or shot, which counter-balances the weight of the piano. It will be noticed that there is a fifth wire secured to the false case. It is run up also over the pulley in the truck, and then off to the side of the stage beyond the side scenes. By pulling this wire the piano is raised or lowered to any desired distance. Counterweights hold the instrument at any position. There is a rope attached to the overhead truck, so that it can be pulled back and forth, thus causing the piano to move across the stage. There are, of course, slits in the ceiling of the mimic stage which allow the wires to pass through.

The lady is raised by a curious device. There is attached to the piano stool a clear piece of plate glass, which comes up through a slot in the stage technically known as a "slider." This glass is made to raise

Fig. 31. The Mystery Explained.

or lower by means of a windlass. The glass rests on a cross-piece of wood and works up and down in a grooved frame, which is secured to a movable truck under the stage. The slot in the stage is continued in the direction in which the glass is to move, and the carpet is of a marked design which will cover the narrow opening.

The bouquet is secured with a thread attached to the piano, and it then goes through the door, where an assistant holds the loose end. A small loop of wire is attached to the bouquet, and a thread runs through it. When the lady enters the room and lays the bouquet on the table, this thread is passed through the loop of wire. When the bouquet is desired to travel to the lady, the assistant has only to raise the end of the thread high enough and the bouquet slides down the incline into the lady's hand.

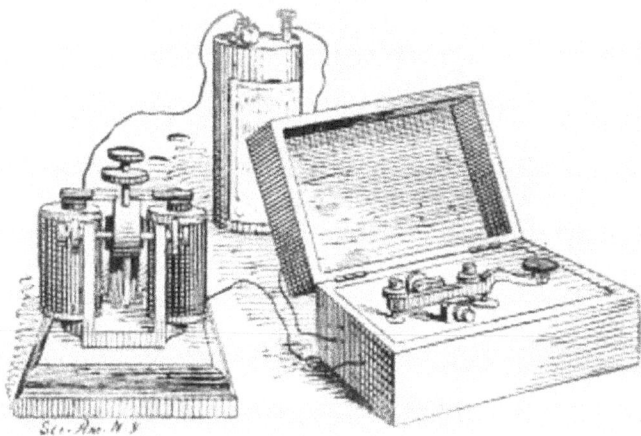

Fig. 32. The Telegraph Set.

A medium in Detroit, Mich., has lately been hoodwinking the public and coining money with an idea that was quite original. He employed a small, shallow box, composed of wooden sides and ends and slate top and bottom. The box and its lid were about of even height, and were hinged together. (Fig. 32.) The box contained a telegraph key connected up to a sounder and a dry battery sitting outside of the box on the table. The medium allowed everything to be well examined. It was proved that the battery on the table was the only means of operating the sounder whenever the key was worked. If one of the wires were disconnected, or the box were closed and the key thus out of the way of manipulation, the sounder would not work. After everything was satisfactorily explained, notes were written on pieces of paper, which were folded and placed upon the table. These are taken, one at a time, and placed in the box and the lid closed. If conditions are favorable, the spirits will be enabled to read one of the inclosed notes, and will send a telegraphic reply over the sounder; and such is ofttimes the result. Of course, we know spirits do nothing of the sort; it is the medium who accomplishes all of this. How does he know the contents of the note? How does he cause the ticker to work with the key inclosed in the box? The visitor is placed on one side of the table, generally facing a window, so as to have the light shine into his or her eyes. The medium sits opposite with his back toward the window; the box containing the key is at his side of the table, with the hinges, or the back of the box, toward the visitor. Now, if the lid of this box is opened and a paper taken off the table and placed in the box and the lid closed, you could not tell for certain if the paper was actually placed in or not, for the simple reason that the cover of the box, when up, completely masked the operation. It is by the above scheme that the medium obtains the notes on the paper. The first one or two are actually placed in the box; then the next one is deliberately dropped into the medium's lap instead of the box. He unfolds it, reads it, refolds it, and, on opening the box, apparently takes it from there and places it back on the table and does not lose track of it. Two or three other papers are placed in it by the visitor, and again taken out by him. Again the visitor is asked to place in it the one the medium knows the contents of. Now the ticker commences to work. With his left hand carelessly resting on the corner of the closed box, the medium writes with his right hand, with a pencil, on a pad of paper, the communication received over the ticker. The visitor removes the paper from the box, and the answer just written by the medium on the pad is found to be a reasonable one to the written request.

All that remains to be explained is the working of the sounder. It is very simple. In the first place, the lid and box are hinged so as to be hinge bound; that is, they will not, of their own weight, quite touch each other, possibly about an eighth of an inch, or less, apart. But by the pressure or weight of the hand they will come together. Now, the telegraph key, like all such instruments, is provided with a tension screw, which can be screwed one way or the other. When the medium desires his instrument to work, he raises this tension screw, to which is fastened the button of the key, just high enough to touch the lid on the inside of the box when it is closed of its own weight. Now, when the hand is resting on the box, he proceeds to make the sounder "speak" at will, with no perceptible movement of his hand. A simple muscular contraction of the palm of the hand, which cannot be detected, is sufficient to control the sensitive key, by pressure of the box cover on it. The whole thing is so simple, and at the same time puzzling, that it makes one laugh to think how little it takes to make a fool of a man.

In the case of this medium, the head of the tension screw was brass, and left a brassy mark on the slate top. He soon observed this, and changed it for a hard rubber one, which left no telltale marks behind. Sometimes he did not raise the tension screw, but laid the folded paper the question was written on on top of it. This made up the required height. Other mediums improved on the above method by working the key through the box by an electro-magnet concealed in the table top. The current to the magnets was turned on and off, or broken, as the line is used, by means of a small button in the body of the table, pressed by the medium's leg. This method allowed him to keep his hand off the box.

The raps, or noises, are produced in various manners. Press your boot heel gently against a table leg. The slipping of the leather against the wood makes perfect spirit raps, wood being a good conductor of sound. The raps apparently come from the table top if attention is directed in that direction. Some mediums, with the tips of their fingers pressed firmly on a table top, slip them, by a dexterous movement, along the varnished surface, thus making very fair examples of raps or thuds. Some mediums, in their own homes, have tables provided with electro-magnets concealed in them, by which the knocks are accomplished. Medical experts claim that a very good result can be obtained by the mere displacement of the tendons of the muscle called *peroneus longus*, in the sheath in which it slides behind the external *malleolus*. Others again produce it by snapping the toe or knee joints. Watch a boy some day as he snaps his finger joints, and if he were to rest his elbows on the table while doing so, the sound would be intensely strengthened.

CHAPTER VI.

SPIRITUALISTIC TIES.

"Ties" have always been one of the great standbys of mediums, second only to slate writing.

The following is a simple test with a rope or piece of string: A long piece of rope is given for inspection, and, on its return to the medium, he coils it up and lays it on the table; the two ends are tied together and sealed fast to the table. The coils of the rope are now allowed to drop on the floor. Lights are lowered, and, in a few minutes, when the lights are relighted, the coil of rope is found with numerous knots tied in it that could not naturally have been accomplished without the ends being untied and unsealed. This mystery is accomplished by simple means. When the medium receives the rope back he does not coil it up as a person would, in the ordinary fashion, but makes the coils so they really form half hitches, and, as he lays them on the table, he runs one of the free ends through all the coils, then ties the two ends together. Each coil will now form an overhand knot. An easy manner of manipulating the rope is as follows: The rope is held in the hands, with palms upward; now, to form the coil, or half hitch, the right hand is given a half twist; this brings the palm facing the person's breast and back of hand outward, and leaves the rope as seen in Fig. 33; this loop is transferred to the left hand (Fig. 34), and the operation repeated until the supply of the rope is exhausted. Now, to make the knots, one end of the rope has simply to be passed through all the loops.

I have seen the above test worked also as follows: Two skeptics were used. One end of the rope was fastened to one of the skeptic's wrists and the other end to the wrist of the second skeptic. The knots were sealed. The rope in this case was quite long, about twenty feet. The medium now makes the rope up into a few coils; out go the lights, and, in a few minutes, on the lights being turned up, the rope is found with knots. This is what happens: When the lights went out, the medium went up to one of the skeptics, and, while talking to him and moving him two or three feet further away from the other skeptic, he has passed the coils over this one man's head, and allowed the coils to drop to the floor. As soon as the skeptic steps out of these, the job is done.

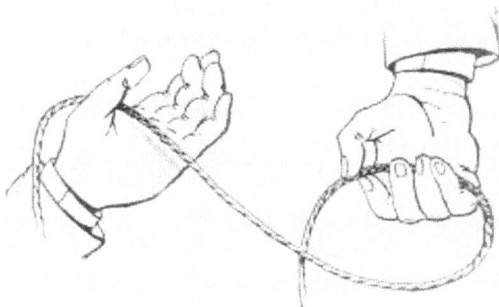

Fig. 33. First Position.

There is another test on somewhat similar lines. A short piece of rope is examined and the performer holds it in one hand and then tosses it into the cabinet, which is empty. On opening the curtain in a few seconds the rope is found with a knot on it. The performer himself actually ties the knot with one hand in the act of tossing the rope

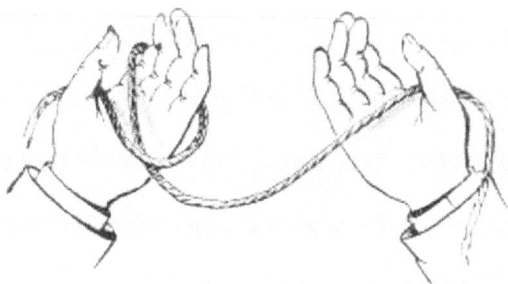

Fig. 34. Second Position.

into the cabinet. The rope is held in the hand palm upward, very near one end, the short end in the hand being with the long end hanging down, the shorter part being between the thumb and the forefinger.

The hand and arm are given a kind of half circular sweep in tossing the rope into the cabinet; this causes the long portion of the rope to swing under, then over the wrist, and across the fingers of the hand. This end is then seized between the fingers and drawn through the loop just made; at the same time the loop is dropped off the wrist as the rope is tossed into the cabinet. In reading the above description it seems like four or five different movements, but with practice they all blend into one.

Here is another test. A single knot is tied in the center of a piece of string; now the ends are tied together and knots sealed. The lights turned down; on their again being turned up, the knot from the center of the cord has disappeared. The moment there was darkness the medium started to work, and kept slipping the knot along the string until it joined the rest at the top of the string, where there is not much fear of its being seen. To further protect himself he uses the following plan: He chews gum colored the same as the sealing wax used. Now in the dark, when he has the single knot up against the others at the end of the string, he covers this knot with part of the chewing gum and blends it in with the sealing wax.

I will now explain a few ties, rope and otherwise, by which the mediums allow themselves to be tied. It is almost invariably the rule for the medium to suggest to the investigator the general way he wishes to be tied. They must have certain conditions, so they say, or the spirits will not work. It is safe to say the conditions are very strict and always in favor of the medium. The female medium has a preference for ties in which tape or muslin, or cotton cloth torn into strips, is utilized. The male performer, as a rule, uses rope and wire. I will first describe what is known as the braid or tape test. Take a piece of tape about three-quarters of an inch wide. Have one end of this securely tied around the wrist; now the person who is conducting the test seats himself in a chair with his hands behind the back of the chair; now have the loose end of the tape passed between the uprights forming the back of the chair; have the other end fastened around the remaining hand. The moment you are in the dark, or hidden from view, you can produce any manifestation that requires the use of one or both hands, by following these instructions. The first hand can be tied as the investigator pleases. Now, when the second hand is to be tied, keep a strain on the tape enough to keep it taut. By so doing a square knot cannot be tied on the tape, but simply a running knot, or a knot around the strand of the tape—a knot that can be slid backward and forward.

Here is what is known as the cotton bandage test. A ring staple or ring screw eye, the ring being about two inches in diameter, is wound around with unbleached muslin of the same color as used to tie the medium's wrists with. This ring is fastened securely into the door jamb or any stationary wooden support by one of the investigators. Two strips of muslin about three feet long are given to the investigator; one of each is tied around one of the medium's wrists and the knots sewed and sealed. Her (for the medium is supposed, in this case, to be a lady) hands are now placed behind her, and the ends of the strips from each wrist are now tied together and the knots tied and also sewed; and what ends are left are evenly cut off near the knots. Another strip of muslin, about the same width and length as the others, is now produced, and one of the committee ties this strip around the knots between her wrists, leaving the ends of equal length. The medium now takes her seat on a small stool, with her back toward the ring in the door jamb. One end of the last muslin strip is passed through the ring and several knots are tied. After tying several knots, the ends of the strips are tacked securely to the woodwork of the door. Another strip is procured and tied around the medium's neck, and then tacked also to the door jamb. Two more strips are now used, one passed around each arm, not tied, and the ends of each tacked to the door. The committee, having done all the work themselves, of course, are thoroughly satisfied as to its genuineness. They now retire from the cabinet, which has been simply made by a curtain across one corner of the room, forming a triangular space. No sooner is the curtain closed than the usual manifestations occur, such as ringing of bells, tooting of horns, banging of tambourine, etc. Immediately the curtain is opened and the medium found securely bound and not a bandage disturbed. Finally a pocket knife is placed upon her lap, the curtain is closed, and in a few seconds the medium comes forward with her bonds cut, but only the wrists separated; this has been done, she claims, by the spirits, with the use of the knife which was placed in her lap. Now to explain away the mystery. In a convenient pocket in her belt she has concealed a small, sharp, open knife, with which she cuts through the bands between the wrists. She cuts this band between the knot on her right wrist and the knot in the middle made by tying the ends of the wrist bands together. She now slips the loop which was tied around off, leaving it whole and still tied around the ring. She is now free to use both hands, and, as the last strips around her arm were not tied, they are easily managed. She makes what manifestations she chooses, and by placing her wrists one each side of the ring, and clasping her hands together, pressing all tightly together, she is ready for examination. The ring being wound with muslin, one cannot see that anything has been changed; and this is the reason it is wound. Another thing to notice is that the spirit cutting is the last test. The reason of this is, if the investigators were to release her, they would discover the secret. Male performers use the same idea for rope ties from which they find it impossible to release themselves. They have a knife blade soldered firmly on to a brass plate, which is riveted or sewed on the back of the performer's trousers, the edge of the knife blade being outward. He has simply to run the rope up and down over this contrivance, and he soon gains his liberty.

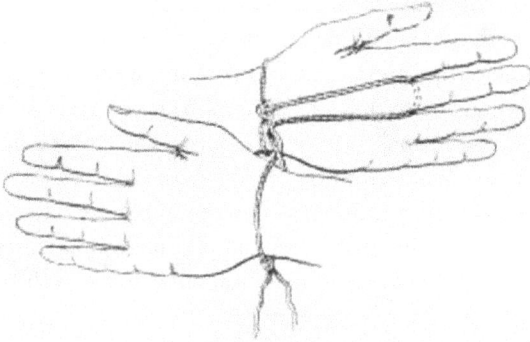

Fig. 35. The Davenport Tie.

I will next illustrate a tie made famous by the Davenport Brothers. (Fig. 35.) The rope used is what is known in trade as a sash rope. Silver Lake or Sampson brand is the best. This is a stiff, polished or smooth, hard finished rope. With this style of rope it is an almost utter impossibility to be tied but what you can free yourself. The Davenports, on first being secured, would try and induce or lead the committee who did the tying to do so in a way which would be advantageous to the medium. See Barnum's "Humbugs of the World," page 136: "The brothers saw they could not wriggle out of the knots. They therefore refused to let the tying be finished." Of course, they did not make the request pointed, or apparent, but, in the coolest natural way, and not suggestive of any conceived plan. Their method was as follows:

One of the committee, holding a piece of rope, about twelve feet long, as near the center as possible, would be requested to tie first one of the medium's left hands, tying two or three good, hard, square knots about the wrist, the knots coming to the inside of the wrist or palm side of the hand. The medium, during this part of the tie, faces the audience. He now explains to the person who does the tying that when he, the medium, places his left hand behind his back, he will place his right hand close against it, and requests the skeptic to tie a few or as many knots on top of that hand as he may see fit. The medium, after this explanation, places his hands behind his back, and then turns around, with his back toward the audience. The committeeman now secures the right hand against the left. The medium now enters the cabinet, is seated in a chair, or on a bench, in which two holes are bored. The ends of the ropes are now passed through these holes, and knots tied in the rope close to the seat of the chair, and thence carried to the front legs of the chair, where it is fastened. Two other smaller ropes are used to tie the medium's legs to the chair. The usual manifestations, such as ringing of bells, tooting of a horn, hands at cabinet window, etc., take place. After this is repeated a few times, the medium comes forth entirely free from the ropes, which he now holds in his hands devoid of knots. Of course, the medium is really the cause of all the demonstrations, and to accomplish the results he must free himself. Now, let us see how it is done. The first hand is tied fair and square, but when he places his two hands behind his back, that's the time the trick is done. In placing his hands behind his back, and before turning around, with back toward the audience, he catches up a little slack of the rope, and, pressing the two hands together, manages not to lose that slack as the two hands are tied together. Another plan is employed so as to be certain not to allow this slack to get away from the medium. In the act of placing the hands behind the back, one part of the rope is allowed to go around the middle finger. The ends are then crossed, A going behind B, before the right hand is placed against left. Of course, the right hand covers the rope, or false tie, completely. When the hand is to be released, the finger has simply to bend down, and off drops the slack part of the rope, and gives plenty of room to draw the hand from the loop. With one hand free, it is easy to produce the desired manifestations, also to release the other hand, and then completely untie the rope. Now, whenever the committee cannot be influenced to tie in the above manner, they are allowed to proceed as they wish. Very few persons can tie a medium securely with the stiff rope furnished. The medium will manage, by slight contortion of his body, to secure a little slack rope, by which agency square knots can be easily upset into a slip or running knot, and, when he fails in this, the rope is deliberately cut with the little knife blade on belt, as described previously. This destroyed rope is now concealed on the medium, and he takes also from his clothes a similar rope and walks out of the cabinet with it, stating the spirits had released him. He again retires to the cabinet, and, in a short time, he is found retied, with his hands behind his back, securely fastened. Here is the explanation:

Fig. 36.
The First Knot.

When he enters the cabinet, he allows both ends of the rope to hang down, holding the rope in center; the rope now, in its doubled condition, has a knot tied near its double end, leaving a knot and loop. (Fig. 36.) Then a single knot, tied in each portion of the rope, each side of this loop knot, far enough away so as to give length enough for the ropes to encircle the wrists, and these single knots come up hard against the loop knot. The ends of the rope are now run through the loop knot, and two loops are thus formed, which can be made larger, as desired, to slip the hands out. (Fig. 37.) The ends of the rope are now run down through holes in the chair seat, and ends fastened, and the medium inserts his wrists in the loop and pulls up taut, and he is

Fig. 37. The Double Loop.

ready for an investigation. It will readily be seen the medium can now do as he pleases, remove his coat, place on a borrowed one, etc.

Another tie frequently used is that in which the medium seats himself in a chair, takes the rope, and ties it around his legs at the knees, with the single knot on top. On this he places his two hands, close together, and has the committee tie his hands with as many knots as they please, from which he nevertheless frees himself. The whole scheme lies in the fact that the medium tied but one knot around the legs, but did not pull it deep into the flesh. When the knots are tied over his hands, he keeps the legs a trifle apart. Now, to release himself, he simply has to draw his legs together, and strain on the ropes, so they sink into the legs a trifle, and let all the slack go above the single knot, thus giving room for the hands to be withdrawn. By forcing the hands apart, the desired slack is easily taken up.

CHAPTER VII.

POST TESTS, HANDCUFFS, COLLARS, ETC.

The "Spiritualistic Post Test" is one of the latest and most successful of mechanical fastenings used by mediums. The most common form is made of what appears to be a piece of joist. This is given to the committee, one of whose members bores a hole through it, near its upper end, and then passes an ordinary rope through the hole, a knot being tied in the rope on each side of the post. The knots are pressed against the post, so that the rope cannot be drawn through the post. The ends of the rope are now unraveled, and the post is fastened to the floor with spikes. The medium is tied to the post by the unraveled ends of the rope. A nail is driven in the top of the post, and a rope is secured to it. This second rope is held by the committee; after the curtains are drawn, bells are rung, etc., showing that the medium has the use of his hands. The trick consists in boring a hole in the center of the end of the joist; a chisel is then inserted in the hole, and the opening is closed with glue and saw-dust tinted with water color. The medium starts the bit, so that there is no danger of the committee boring the hole too low, or so high that it will strike the chisel. When the nail is driven in, it forces the chisel down and cuts the rope. The medium may now ring bells, etc. After he is through ringing the bells, he puts back the ends of the rope in the post.

There is another very good rope and mechanical post test sometimes used by mediums. A post in an upright position is securely fastened to the floor. In the upper part of the post a hole is bored clear through, to allow of two small ropes being passed through the opening from side to side. The medium passes the ropes through the post, then invites the committee to tie his hands fast against the post, and then to tie or nail the ends of the rope down on the floor. All the usual manifestations take place. The medium is also instantaneously released, and rope and knots are found undisturbed. By glancing at Fig. 38 the mystery will be cleared up. The post is hollow, and carries a leaden or iron weight. This weight has a horizontally extending passage to correspond with the channel in the post. This weight is held in the top part of the post by a catch, which is released by a projecting bolt-head at the bottom of the post. It will be remembered that the

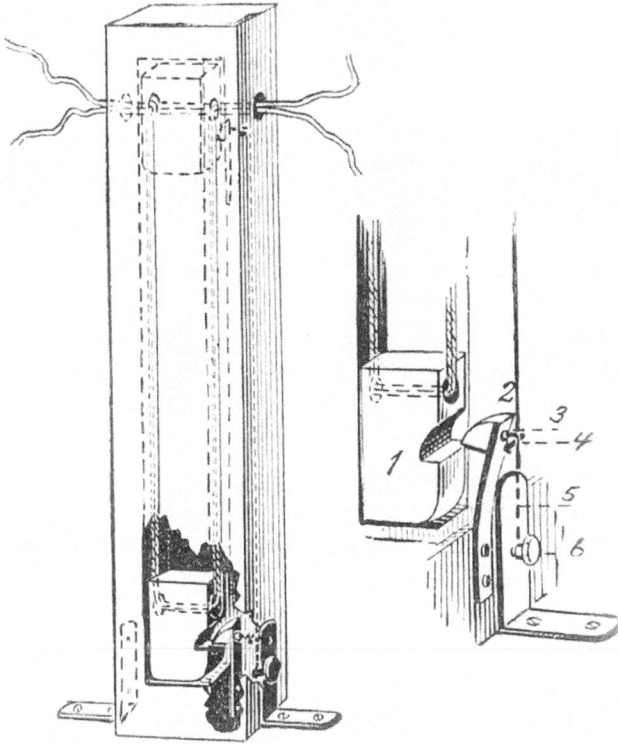

Fig. 38. The Trick Post.

1. Lead weight with notch.
2. Spring catch.
3. Hole in catch by which cord is secured.
4. Roller over which cord, 5, runs; cord is attached at one end, 3, to spring catch, and at other end at 6 to bolt in angle piece.

post is made fast to the floor by screws passing through angle irons fastened by bolts to the post. It is one of these bolt-heads that releases the catch. At the bottom of the post is another catch, which will also hold the weight at the bottom. The one bolt will release both catches. The medium runs the ropes through the post, releases the catch, which allows weight to drop, carrying ropes with it; and the catch locks the weight at the bottom of the post. They can now tie the medium. All he has to do is to release the weight; he can then pull the rope up and get as large a slack as he desires, allowing the weight to drop back again. There is a chair—an ordinary-looking wooden kitchen chair—worked on somewhat the same style. There is a hole bored through each rear leg or upright of the back. The medium sits on the chair, facing the back of it, and has a hand tied to each upright. The slack is obtained the same as in the post, with the exception that a spring instead of a weight is used, and it is locked or released by the backward or forward sliding of a portion of the chair-seat.

A convincing trick often employed is the iron ring test. The medium and investigator sit opposite each other, clasping their hands. An iron ring is now placed on the medium's lap, and the cabinet door is closed; in a few moments the door is opened again, and the ring is found on the investigator's arm, although he has never released his hold of the medium's hand. The medium has concealed in his coat sleeve a duplicate of the ring used. When the cabinet door is closed, the medium spreads his legs apart, allowing the ring to drop on the seat of his chair, the bottom of which should be of cane or of cloth, in order to avoid the noise due to the dropping of the ring. He now replaces his legs, and, of course, this ring is hidden merely by his sitting on it. The ring in his sleeve he tosses on to the skeptic's arm, and, of course, without the hands being unclasped.

The handcuff trick is always a great favorite with the medium. He has no objection to placing his hands in any pair of handcuffs furnished by the audience. A few moments after he has entered the cabinet, he begins throwing out various articles of clothing; but, on examination, the handcuffs are found to be still on his wrists. It is impossible to see how he could have taken off his coat. As a final test the medium comes out of the cabinet holding the handcuffs in his hand still locked. There are only a few styles of handcuffs made, and all the medium has to do is to secure the proper key for each style. He conceals these keys on his person, and by the aid of his fingers and teeth the proper key can be fitted to the handcuffs. It is impossible, with some types of handcuffs, to get the fingers to the keyhole. If such a pair are placed on the performer, and he cannot use his teeth to hold the key, he slips the key into a convenient crack in the cabinet or in the chair. The lock of the handcuffs being forced on to the key, the handcuffs can then be readily unlocked.

The spirit collar is also a favorite instrument of the medium. It consists of a brass collar which fits closely about the performer's neck. Through the openings in the end of the collar, is placed a chain. After the collar is on the performer's neck, the chain is placed around a post and carried back and through the padlock used to lock the collar. By this arrangement the performer is securely fastened to a post; but after he is concealed by the use of any convenient means, he suddenly appears before the audience minus the collar, while the collar will be found locked, as before. The trick depends for its success on the series of bolts with which the collar is studded. The bolts, with one exception, are all false, being pieces of metal simply screwed into the top and bottom of the collar, and not penetrating through them. One bolt, however, passes through the collar and engages the two parts thereof; the parts terminate in a tongue which fits in the socket in the other half of the collar. The bolt passes through this tongue so accurately that there is no danger of its being removed with the fingers. The performer uses a small wrench to remove the bolt.

There are numerous other devices, such as trick bolts, which are inserted by a spectator through a post and screwed up tight, the medium being fastened to the bolt. He has simply to give the bolt a half twist, usually toward the right, and the bolt comes apart. The joint is invisible to the eye, and, in fact, is made more so just before it is used each time by being rubbed with sandpaper, which slightly roughens the bolt, making the joint imperceptible to the naked eye. There are staples, ordinary looking staple-plates, which are apparently screwed fast into the bench on which the medium is seated. The hands of the medium are fastened to the staples by wire. The staples are not fastened to the plates by riveting them, as is ordinarily done, but are held by a spring catch, concealed under the plate, and working in a notch in the staple. This is released by the medium's pushing the catch back by the insertion of a piece of clock spring between the staple plate and the bench. After releasing himself he performs the stereotyped manifestations, and at the finish has simply to jam the staples back into their plate, whereupon they are locked or held fast by the spring catch or bolt. This was a device used by a Boston medium.

There are also trick bags in which the medium is bound up or tied. In one style of bag there is a string running in the selvage, or turned-over portion of the bag at the top. As the string is about to be drawn taut the medium inserts one of his fingers into a portion of this selvage not sewn, and pulls down enough slack of the cord to allow him, after the tying, either to place his arm through or to get out entirely. Another style is this: The medium has a round wooden plug, covered with cloth like the bag. This he has concealed about him. As the mouth of the bag is gathered together to tie the string, the medium inserts this plug, and bag and plug are both tied. After the tying he has simply to remove the plug and he can then place his hand through and release the cord, or shove it off the bag completely. Still another way is to have a duplicate bag concealed down one trousers leg and coming up at the back of the neck under the coat, the mouth of the bag being upward. When the medium gets in, his manager or the director of the séance gathers the mouth of the bag together, and, at the same time, pulls the duplicate bag out from under the medium's coat. He pulls this up four or five inches higher than the original bag and ties his handkerchief around where the two bags are joined, so the trick will not be detected. He then allows a committee to tie, and even sew, the bag together—of course, the duplicate, not the first one. The medium has simply to pull the first bag down around him, get out of it and conceal it on his body. A "dodge" used sometimes is to borrow one of the investigators' handkerchiefs and drop it into the duplicate bag; and, after the medium has escaped and the bag is given for inspection, the bag is opened and the handkerchief found inside. This strengthens the effect of the trick, inasmuch as it convinces the onlookers that the medium certainly must have been got out by the aid of spirits, as the handkerchief—a very small article, in comparison to the body of the medium—could not be removed until the string had been released from the bag.

Mediums are great judges of human nature; they know full well the usual action of the human mind, the direction the thoughts are liable to travel in. This is part of their stock-in-trade—to try to do just such things as the handkerchief "dodge," in order to convince the skeptic of the truth of the wonders witnessed.

CHAPTER VIII.

SÉANCES AND MISCELLANEOUS SPIRIT TRICKS.

A test which made the Eddy Brothers famous was their "light" and "dark" séances. Horatio Eddy gave what he termed a "light séance," and William was famous for the "dark séance." Instead of using a cabinet of wood, Horatio formed one simply by stretching a couple of shawls or curtains across a corner of the room, thus making a triangular inclosure. A table containing the usual musical instruments, bells, tambourine, guitar, etc., is placed in this space. The medium sits on a chair in front of this curtain, to the left hand side. Next to him, on his right, sits a gentleman selected from the audience, and to the right of this gentleman, a lady similarly chosen. William Eddy now pins across the breasts of the two gentlemen a third shawl, attaching the ends to the curtain. (Fig. 39.) Previously to this, however, Horatio has grasped with both his hands the gentleman's left arm; the lady is requested to grasp the gentleman's right arm. In this position neither can make a movement but what one of the others would be immediately cognizant of it. Presently there is a commotion among the articles on the table behind the screen; they appear floating in the air above the top of the curtains, some coming through and tapping the trio on the head. A hand comes through the curtain and writes a message on the slate held by William Eddy. Numerous other tests are performed—all in subdued light, not darkness. Now, to raise the veil from this mystery: In grasping the left arm of the person in the center, the medium first grasps the gentleman's left arm with his, the medium's, left hand, fingers being spread apart as far as possible. With this hand he presses quite hard, and takes a light hold of the same arm, but above the left hand. If the medium gently and carefully removes the right hand, the action cannot, by sense of touch, be detected. Sometimes, so as to enable him to use both hands, another ruse is also employed. A piece of heavy sheet lead is

Fig. 39. The Light Séance.

cut in the shape of the medium's hand. This is placed in his left hand. With this hand he grasps the skeptic's arm. Being made of lead, the hand easily conforms or bends to the shape of the arm, and, what is more, if the real hand of the medium be quietly removed, the leaden hand remains behind, giving the same sense of touch as if the actual hand were there. (Fig. 40.) Of course, with the hands free, the medium can stealthily glide between the curtains, grasp and manipulate the instruments, and throw them to the floor, immediately replacing his hands gently.

A rather clever test used in a dark séance, given by Miss Annie Eva Fay, is one in which the hands are not bound. Miss Fay made cotton, bandage and tape-ties a success, and sometimes varied her séance by not using a tie, but by continually clapping her hands together during the darkness. She also had her mouth filled with water. Nevertheless, the usual manifestations occurred. The horn "tooted," the tambourine and guitar floated, bells rang, etc. The dodge she employed was this: Instead of clapping her hands together, she slapped one against her forehead, which gave the same sound, and gave her one hand at liberty. She also swallowed the water. She was now at liberty to blow the horn, ring bells or the like. When she was finished, she refilled her mouth with water from a bottle concealed on her person, and again resumed, clapping her hands together instead of striking one hand against her forehead. An investigator suspected the idea of the water and once came prepared with a glass of milk, which he requested the medium to use instead. She consented. The horn tooted just the same, and the medium's mouth still contained the milk. She had simply inserted the end of the horn in one of her nostrils. Another time she merely emptied the liquid into one of the hand bells on the table and held it upside down in her lap. Still another "wrinkle" is the use of a rubber ball with a hole in it. This can readily be attached to the horn, and squeezing the ball does the tooting.

Dr. Henry Slade was, of course, identified and recognized as the principal slate-writing medium, but at various times he presented other phenomena, one of which was the playing of an accordion while held in one hand under the table. The accordion was taken by him from the table with his right hand, at the end containing the strap, the keys or notes at the other end being away from him. He thus held the accordion beneath the table, and his left hand was laid on top of the table, where it was always in plain view. Nevertheless, the accordion was heard to give forth melodious tunes, and at the conclusion was brought up on top of the table as held originally; the whole

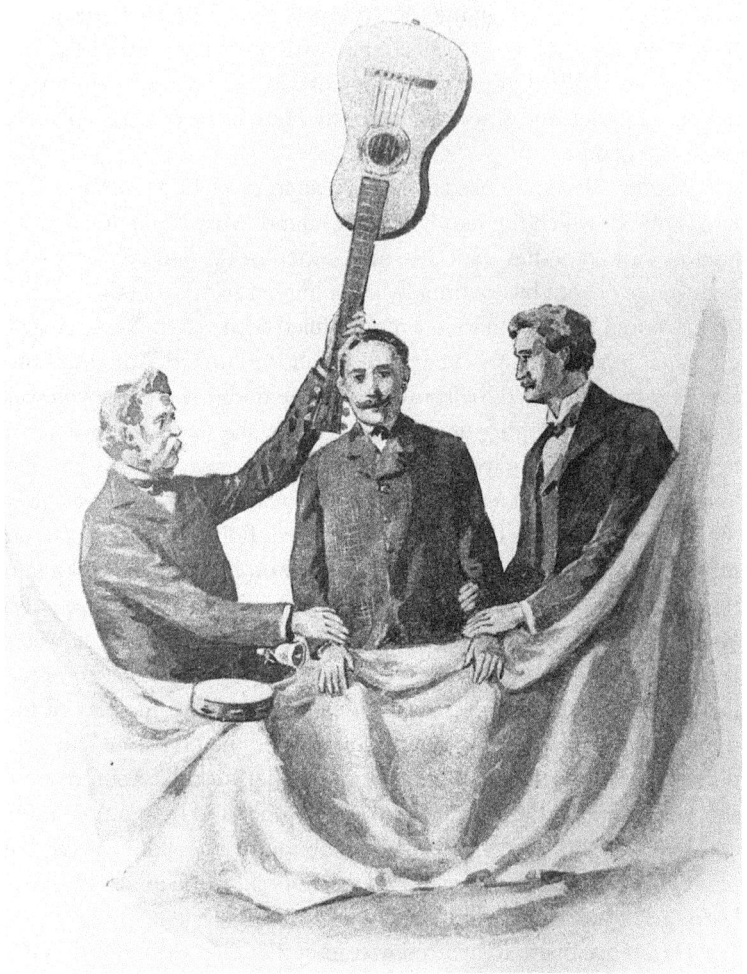

Fig. 40. The Mystery Explained.

dodge consisting in turning the accordion end for end as it went under the table. The strap end being now downward, and held between
the legs, the medium's hand grasped the keyboard end, and worked
the bellows and keys, holding the accordion firmly with the legs and
working the hand, not with an arm movement, but mostly by a simple wrist movement. Of course, at the conclusion, the hand grasped

the accordion at the strap end, and brought it up in this condition. Sometimes an accordion is tied with strings and sealed so the bellows cannot be worked. This is for the dark séance. Even in this condition the accordion is played by inserting a tube in the air-hole or valve and by the medium's using his lungs as bellows.

In regard to dark séances and materializations, I would state that they are so barefaced and bold it is hardly worth while to worry about them. What cannot be done in the dark? Spirit costumes, to be donned later by the medium to impersonate people from the other world, are concealed in strange places under the very eyes of the investigators—in the body of the guitar, in a drum, about the person of one of the circle of skeptics, who is really a confederate, or behind the surface of a wall. Time and place make all the difference in the method of work used by mediums. In their homes mediums have any number of accomplices, who enter the room under cover of darkness by various means—one way, by means of a trap in the floor. This opens upwardly; the carpet does not have to be cut, and can also be well tacked down. The trap is not cut square, but triangularly, across the two sides of the room in one corner. Through this trap the confederates, disguised as spirits, enter from the cellar below and vanish. Another method is to gain admittance from an adjoining room. Between the two rooms are sliding doors, misnamed "folding" doors. The space in one of the walls is not only large enough to receive its own single door, but also a portion of the other. Before commencing the séance, the doors are locked and the key kept by a committee. The doors are also sealed with court plaster across their joints, and said court plaster sealed with sealing-wax. The confederates are not obliged to push the doors apart; they simply slide both at the same time toward the side previously mentioned. This side receives one door and a portion of the other, thus leaving an opening for a person slyly to creep through.

Sometimes, in the circle of investigators, there are five or six confederates. Three of these are placed or seated together. Now, if all in the circle join hands, it seems no one could assist the medium without the fact being discovered; but in the center, one of three confederates, sitting together, releases the hands of his companions, and, in the dark, "cuts up" all the tricks he wishes and returns to the circle again,

no one being any the wiser. Of course, if one confederate were seated between two of the skeptics, he would not dare let go his hands;
but when a friend is placed each side of him, it makes no difference.
A test often used, when everybody, medium included, is sitting at a
table, is the wire test. A copper wire is threaded through the shirt
sleeve of every male member present, and through the sleeve of the
ladies' dresses, the wire being fastened to the table by staples. When
the lights are put out, the spirits "raise Cain" again. It is the medium
again. The wire did not go through his shirt sleeves, but through two
short extra shirt sleeves, or cuffs, which he wears over the real sleeves.
All he has to do is to slip out of these, produce the manifestations, and
slip back into the cuffs again.

Fig. 41. Ground Plan of Cabinet.

A test that caused more talk and wonderment than all the rest
of the cabinet tricks combined is the chair and net test. The medium
enters a very small cabinet, just large enough to contain him when
sitting down in a chair. The cabinet is closed by a single door, locked
with a padlock, the keyhole of which is sealed; the door is also sealed
all around the edges. A fish-net so finely meshed that even the finger of the medium could not be pushed through, is now placed over
this cabinet and tacked to it all around the bottom. This miniature
cabinet is set in the cabinet proper, and a chair, with the usual bell,
tambourine, etc., placed beside it. Doors are closed, and immediately the fun begins. Bells, tambourine, and horns all play together. A
sudden fall of the chair and instruments is heard, and the cabinet
doors being opened, everything is found strewn about; the smaller
cabinet is, however, still found as it was left, with the netting over it
and seals undisturbed. Again the large cabinet is closed, and almost
immediately it is opened from the inside, and out walks the medium;
and the netting on the smaller cabinet is examined once more, and
likewise the padlock and seals, everything is found intact. The whole
trick depends upon the construction of the smaller cabinet. Fig. 41

represents a ground plan of the apparatus. The floor is not nailed or fastened to the sides. There are four battens or strengthening pieces, one in each corner of the cabinet, running from top to bottom; these are securely fastened to the floor, but not to the sides of the cabinet. Over these battens is laid a strip of wood that is really made fast to the cabinet. This leaves in each corner a socket or pocket the height of the cabinet, and in these work, telescopic fashion, the four battens which are made fast to the bottom. The bottom is set inside of the cabinet, not on the outside. It is only tacked to the sides of the bottom of cabinet. It will now be readily observed that the medium has only to stand up in order to raise the main part of the cabinet quite a height above the bottom, as seen at Fig. 42. It is held in the above position by a concealed catch. The medium can now produce manifestations, and, as he is about to drop the cabinet back into the bottom, he gives the leg of the chair a jerk and over it goes, and down drops the cabinet. There is also a catch that automatically locks the bottom firm to the cabinet, so as to allow inspection of the same.

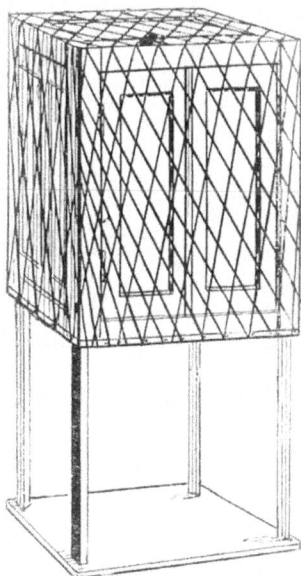

Fig. 42. The Trick Cabinet.

The above manifestation was in use long before the wire cage test, and is considered by some mediums more convincing than the latter. While speaking about the wire cage test, I may as well describe one form of it. There are numerous makes, but the one explained will serve as a sample of the rest. A cage composed of uprights and cross-bars of iron is made fast to an iron frame containing a small door through which the medium enters. Sometimes the door is done away with and the bottom of the cage is separated from it. The medium sits on this bottom, and the cage is lifted and placed over him. The bottom and cage are padlocked together or bound with wires and sealed.

Fig. 43. The Wire Cage.

No matter what method is used, the results are the same; the medium can play the instruments or escape, as he may see fit. The wire cage is, we shall say, of a design similar to that shown in Fig. 43. There is no door to it, and the cage being secured by a wire bottom padlocked on or nailed fast to the floor. A close inspection of Fig. 44 will help to expose the fraud. The lower cross-bar is not riveted through the frame at its end, but ends square against it, and a false rivet head, having no connection with it, is riveted on the frame where this cross-bar is supposed to emerge. All of the upright rods are made fast only to this cross-bar. In the other cross-bars they simply go through holes, not closely, but loosely, to ensure then to be slid up and down. The tops of these rods are riveted, but not made fast to the frame at the top. The center rod is not made permanent in the lower cross-bar, but is fastened so it can be turned around one way or the other. Now, where all these rods are supposed to come through the lower part of

Fig. 44. The Cage Opened.

the iron frame are rivet-heads representing the heads of the rods, should they have come through. The bottom frame is drilled half way through for the end of each rod to enter a little, the middle rod is tapped with a thread like a screw on its end, and its corresponding hole is also tapped. It will now be seen why this rod was left to turn. By pulling cross-bar down and then screwing this middle rod tight, everything is solid; but unscrew the rod and raise the cross-bar, and all the upright rods will travel with it and the medium is at liberty. And we have another spirit mystery laid bare. I could describe numerous other tricks and devices of a like nature, but a few are as good as a quantity; sufficient, in fact, to place the investigator on his guard against being duped by like contrivances.

I believe a few words in regard to spirit photography will not be amiss. These are made or produced in various ways: First, a glass with an image on it of the desired spirit form could be placed in the plate holder, in front of the sensitive plate, so that the image on the glass would act on the sensitive plate. The size and distinctness of the re-sulting spirit form would vary according to the distance between the two plates. Second, a figure clothed in white can be introduced for a moment behind the sitter and then be withdrawn before the sitting is over, leaving a shadowy image on the plate. Third, a microscopic picture of the spirit form can be inserted in the camera box alongside of the lens, and by a small magnifying lens its image can be thrown on the sensitive plate with that of the sitter. This is the trick used when the skeptic brings his own plate for the negative. Fourth, a glass with the spirit image can be placed behind the sensitive plate after the sitting is completed, and afterward, by a feeble light, the image can be impressed upon the plate with that of the sitter. Fifth, the silver nitrate bath could have a glass side, and the image impressed by a secret light while the glass plate apparently was being coated with the sensitive film. Sixth, the spirit form can be printed first on the nega-tive and then the living sitter by a second printing, or the spirit can be printed on the paper and the sitter's portrait printed over it. Seventh, a sensitive plate can be prepared by what is known as the dry process, the spirit form being impressed on it; and then, at a subsequent time, the portrait of the living sitter can be taken on this same plate, so that the two will develop together. Eighth, take a solution of sulphate of quinine and paint on the background screen a picture of any one; when it dries it is invisible to the naked eye. Still, when the picture is taken, the painted picture is very plainly seen on the glass negative.

Ninth, small pictures are taken on thin, transparent celluloid and fastened against the front lens of the camera, and when the photograph is taken the picture appears. Of course, the above are by no means all the methods, but enough to illustrate the possibilities of obtaining two pictures on the same plate or at one sitting.

CHAPTER IX.

MISCELLANEOUS TRICKS.

The "Magician's Omelette."

The magician has never proved himself an adept at the art of cooking, from an epicure's standpoint; yet the ease with which he can bake cakes in borrowed hats and cook omelettes in empty pans has long been a source of wonder to the economical housewife, as well as to the professional cook.

To see the magician hold a small, shallow, empty pan over the blaze of a spirit lamp for a few moments, when an omelette, done to a turn, appears in the pan and is cut up and distributed to the audience, one is almost convinced that at least one person has solved that most perplexing of all problems—how to live without work.

But has he solved it? No! my friend, no more than you or I. He has merely deceived you; but most cleverly, you must admit.

The pan is without any preparation whatever; but as much cannot be said of the wand, which he is continually stirring around in the pan. This wand is hollow, with an opening at one end only; and in the wand, previous to the trick, of course, are placed the properly seasoned ingredients of an omelette, after which the end is closed with a metal plug that is turned and enameled to correspond with the opposite end of the wand.

When the pan is being examined the performer is holding the wand in his hand, and such an innocent-appearing black stick is never suspected of being in any way connected with the trick. Just before holding the pan over the lamp the performer finds it a most easy matter to remove the plug from the end of the wand, when, by holding the wand by the closed end, he can empty the contents into the pan in the mere act of passing the open end of the wand around the inside of the pan. (Fig. 45.)

Fig. 45. The "Magician's Omelette."

The metal of which the pan is made being thin, and there not being a great quantity of the omelette, assisted by a large flame from the lamp, it only requires a few moments to cook the omelette, when it is turned out on a plate and carried down to the audience.

It is hardly necessary to say that when the cooked omelette is carried down, the wand is left on the stand, which prevents any inquisitive person asking to see it.

Spinning and Balancing Tricks.

The spinning handkerchief is a great favorite with jugglers. A handkerchief is borrowed, thrown in the air and caught on the end of a whirling stick held by the juggler, when the handkerchief spreads out to its full size and commences to spin around rapidly. The secret is that in the end of the stick a needle is inserted about one-quarter of an inch, leaving the sharp end out. When the handkerchief is caught on the end of the whirling stick the needle point passes through it, thus preventing its falling off the stick, which is rapidly whirled around, and the handkerchief will spread out and spin about on the end of the stick.

Fig. 46. The Spinning Handkerchief.

Jugglers are very partial to tricks performed with eggs, and spinning an egg on its smaller end is a trick they are almost sure to perform. It is impossible to spin a raw egg; so our juggler uses a hard-boiled one, and spins it on its small end in a shallow japanned tray. If the tray is kept gently moving in a small circle in the opposite direction to that in which the egg is spinning, the latter will continue to spin as long as desired. (Fig. 47.)

The egg spinning trick is usually followed by a balancing trick in which a playing card is balanced upon a small wand, and an egg is then balanced on a corner of the card. This trick usually calls forth a great pretension of skill on the part of the performer, when, in reality, no skill whatever is required.

The wand is of ebony, or some dark wood, and about three inches from one end is a small hole. The egg is made of wood, painted white, and with a small hole in one end. The card is composed of two

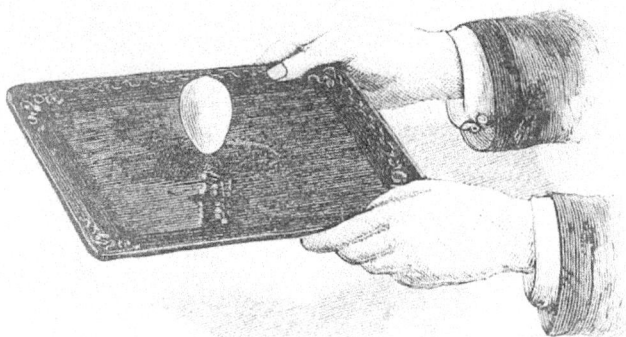

Fig. 47. Spinning an Egg.

cards glued together, with a fine steel wire between them, running diagonally from corner to corner of the card, with the ends of the wire projecting about a quarter of an inch. The prepared egg is on a plate with several ordinary eggs, and the card is placed on a pack of common cards. The wand is held in one hand, the card taken in the other and apparently balanced on one corner on the wand; but in reality the wire point is placed in the hole in the wand. Now the assistant passes the prepared egg to the juggler, who carefully balances it upon the corner of the card; that is, slips the hole in the end of the egg over the wire point projecting from the card.

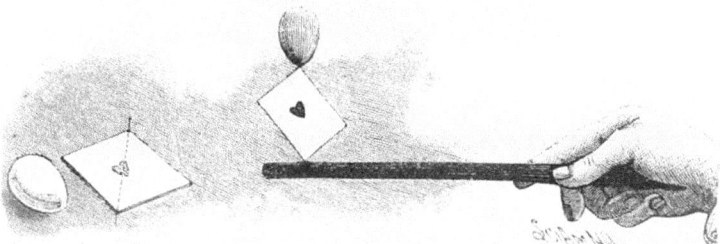

Fig. 48. Balancing Card and Egg on Wand.

A fitting finale to such a juggling act is that in which a potato is placed on the hand of the assistant and cut in two with a sharp sword, without leaving any mark upon the skin. As a general thing, a second potato is then cut upon the throat of the assistant. This apparently marvelous mastery of the sword always brings forth great applause.

Fig. 49. Cutting a Potato on the Hand.

Among the several medium-sized sound potatoes on a tray are placed two potatoes prepared as follows: Insert a needle crosswise of the potato near the bottom. After showing the sword to be really sharp, by cutting paper and slicing one or two of the potatoes, the performer picks up one of the prepared potatoes and places it on the assistant's hand; but apparently it does not lie to suit him, so he slices off one side of it, using care to cut away the side just under the needle and as close to it as possible, then places the potato once again on the assistant's hand. After making a few flourishes with the sword, he cuts through the potato, dividing it in half. (Fig. 49.)

In striking the potato with the sword he makes sure that the sword will come exactly crosswise on the needle; consequently, when the sword reaches the needle it can go no farther, and the brittle nature of the potato will cause it to fall apart, the very thin portion below the needle offering no resistance to the separation. The second potato is then cut in the same manner on the assistant's neck. There are many other false juggling tricks, but the above will suffice to show that "there are tricks in all trades but yours."

The Blindfolded Juggler.

While watching the clever manner in which a good juggler passes various articles from hand to hand, how many people ever give a
thought to the many hours of practice devoted to even the simples
trick that he performs? To become even a passable juggler, many
weary months of constant practice are necessary. There are tricks
in all trades, and some of the most successful entertainers in this line
can scarcely do a half dozen genuine feats of juggling, yet they are
great favorites with the public. It has been truly said that "the tricks

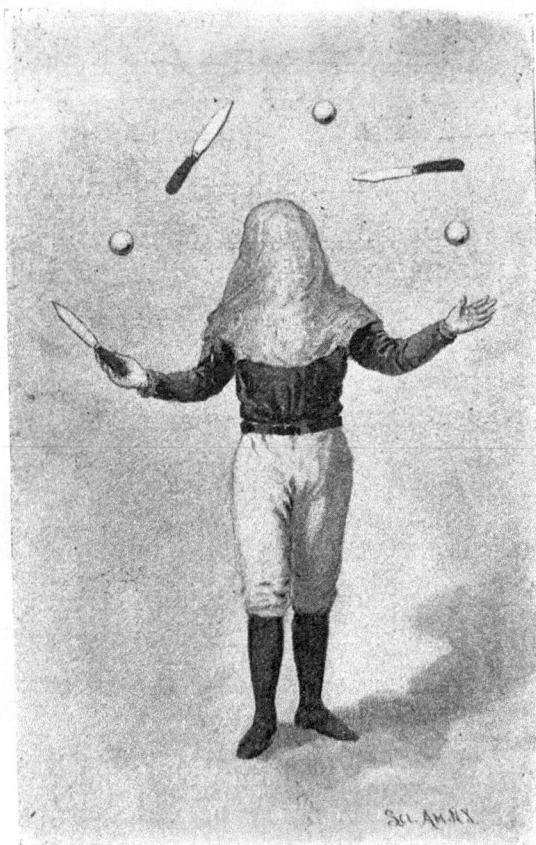

Fig. 50. The Blindfolded Juggler.

that require the most practice are the least appreciated by the average spectator." It is our intention merely to show how a simple trick has won fame for several well-known jugglers.

This is the trick of juggling blindfolded. An assistant tightly binds a heavy handkerchief over the juggler's eyes, and then, to make sure that he cannot see, there is placed over his head and shoulders a sort of bag, made of heavy goods, which should exclude all light, even if his eyes were not tightly bound with the handkerchief. Regardless of this, the juggler performs the usual passes with balls and knives. Yet, when the bag is removed, the bandage over his eyes is found undisturbed. (Fig. 50.)

The explanation is simple. The bag is made of the usual coarse bagging, and a few threads are pulled out of the part that will come in front of the juggler's face when the bag is over his head, thus allowing him to see between the remaining threads as though looking through a coarse screen. (Fig. 51.)

When the bag is being placed over his head, and during the seeming effort of passing the arms through the armholes in the bag, the performer or assistant has no trouble in pushing the handkerchief up from the eyes to the forehead, thus allowing him to see through the open work of the bag. In removing the bag after the act, there is no trouble in pulling the handkerchief down over the eyes.

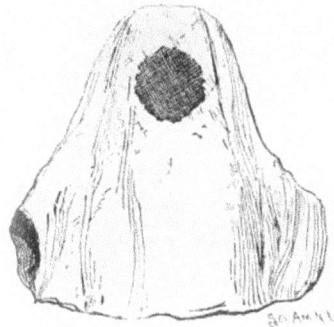

Fig. 51. The Illusion Explained.

The Chinese Rods and Cords.

Nothing excites curiosity in the public mind more than a simple and clever puzzle, and the "Fifteen Puzzle" and "Pigs in Clover" have given enjoyment to hundreds of thousands. The Chinese rods and cords, which forms the subject of our engravings, is in the line of ingenious inventions, and is really more in the nature of a trick than a toy. (Fig. 52.)

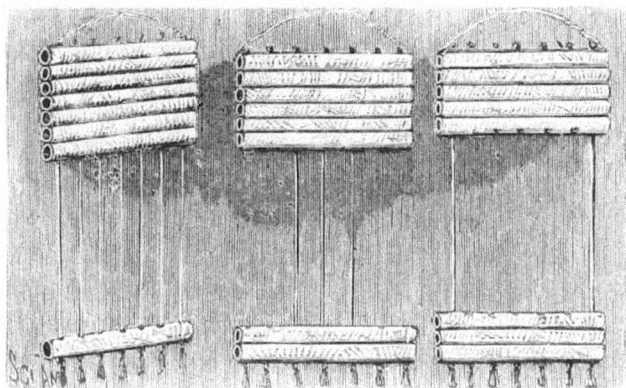

Fig. 52. Chinese Rods and Cords.

It is of Chinese origin, and the example shown in our engraving was purchased in Chinatown, San Francisco, Cal. The puzzle consists of eight pieces of bamboo or hollow ivory tubes, each containing seven holes spaced equidistantly. Through these holes are seen to pass seven silken cords, each with a bead at the top and a tassel at the bottom. The toy is held by the loop at the top, which serves to hold the upper rod. When it is first picked up, its condition is shown in our first engraving at the left. There are seven of the rods at the top and one at the bottom. Now the lower bar of the upper set is moved down to the bar at the bottom; the two lower bars will appear to be supported by three cords at the center, as shown in our engraving, four of the cords having vanished. If the next bar is brought down, another change is observed, only the two outer cords being seen. This is shown to the right of our engraving. If the next bar is brought down, the end cords have approached the center, and five of the seven cords have vanished. The next rod brought down brings five cords into view, the two end ones and the center one being visible. When the next bar is pulled down, the center and the outer cords only remain; so that, if all

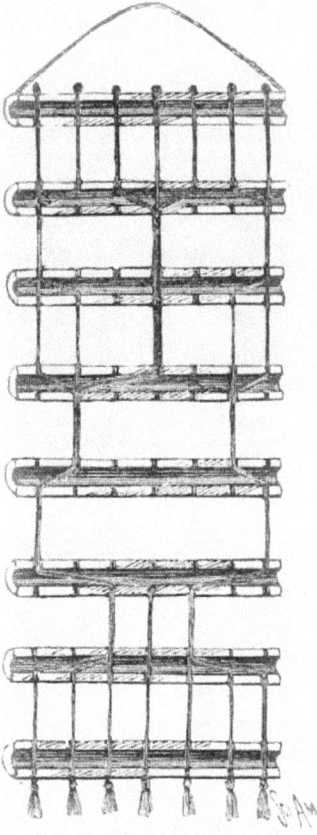

Fig. 53. The Illusion Explained.

the bars between the top and bottom bars are brought together, the seven cords appear to pass entirely through them. Fig. 53 gives a clew to the mystery. The rods are all hollow, and each contains seven holes; and our engraving shows the course of the silk cords. It will be noticed that where a number of cords pass through a single hole, the strand which is formed is much thicker than are the single cords; as they are of different colors, the effect is most pleasing. It will be observed that the strings go clear through the top bar; but in the next bar, although they enter the seven holes at the top, they emerge from three holes at the bottom, three of the strands going through the center hole and two through each of the end holes, and so on throughout the entire number of bars, the strings changing their course, as is clearly shown in our engraving, thus causing the increase and decrease in their number.

The "Surprise" Pen.

Our engraving shows a very clever trick pen which would tend to create great surprise among the uninitiated. Let us suppose that a gentleman is seated at his desk and is busily writing when a neighbor comes in, and he jokingly challenges the latter to try and forge his signature. He hands the pen to his friend, who attempts to write. Immediately there is an explosion, and the paper receives a big ink blot. The writer is apt to be surprised by the report, which is like a pistol shot, and, if a timid person, is apt to be frightened. The noise comes from the pen itself, as it is so constructed that it can be loaded and shot off at will. The person in the secret can handle the pen with safety, but the poor unfortunate will experience a rather unexpected shock to his nerves when he attempts to write with it.

Fig. 54. The "Surprise" Pen.

The upper part of the penholder, into which an ordinary writing pen is thrust, works on a pivot about half way down its length. This separate part is provided with only one-half a bottom, in order that it may engage the conical head of a piston rod, which ends in a plunger, which sets off the cap secured in the bottom of the penholder. The normal position of the plunger is against the cap of the holder; but it can be raised by means of a projecting pin riveted to the rod and passing through a slot cut in the side of the lower part of the holder. Now, the closed half of the bottom of the pivoted end enters a notch caused by the conical head of the plunger; and the plunger, with its spring, is cocked, as it were, by means of the projecting pin, and is held in place by the bottom of the pivoted section. When the pen is pressed to the paper the pivoted section swings on the pivot, releasing the plunger, which is forced down on the explosive cap by the spring.

The lower end of the penholder is threaded, so that it can secure the end cap firmly in place. The explosive cap is put in the end cap, and it is screwed on the bottom of the holder. Ordinary paper caps for children's pistols are used. As long as the plunger simply rests on the cap there is no danger of an explosion; but, just before the joker wishes to give his friend a scare, he cocks it by pushing the plunger up with the pin, until the pivoted top engages it.

The "Miraculous Wineglasses."

As a rule, magicians are very generous fellows, always ready to give their audiences something, such as coins and handkerchiefs, but,

Fig. 55. The "Miraculous Wineglass."

just when one thinks they have the gift safely in their grasp, it mysteriously vanishes. However, there are a few exceptions to this rule, one of whom is a very popular English performer.

This magician goes among the audience and borrows a gentleman's handkerchief, and immediately produces from it a glass filled with sherry. This he offers to the ladies, then, shaking the handkerchief, he produces a second glass full of port for the gentlemen, next one of ginger beer for the younger members, and one of milk for the very young, but there being

Fig. 56. The Glass Covered with Rubber.

present one or two teetotalers, he next produces a glass of water, and lastly a glass of stout for himself. All of these are pronounced by the audience to be excellent.

The glasses are of the small stem wineglass pattern. On both sides of the magician's coat, inside, of course, are large pockets, and in each pocket is placed in a prearranged form three of the glasses. To prevent a possible spilling of their contents (and, as each glass is filled to the brim, this would be very difficult), there is fastened over the mouth of each glass a thin soft rubber cap or cover, as shown in the small engraving.

To produce the glass, the performer spreads the borrowed handkerchief, which should be a large one, over his breast in such a manner that one hand is concealed under it; and with this hand he reaches in the pocket and brings forth the proper glass, removing the rubber cover and leaving it in the pocket. This move is repeated until all the glasses have been brought out. After producing three of the glasses with, say, the left hand, he must spread the handkerchief so as to cover the right hand, leaving the left one free to manipulate the handkerchief, as it would be most awkward to try and produce the glasses from both sides of the coat with the same hand.

Fig. 57. The Miraculous Wine Bottle.

This trick is a most effective one, as the spectators cannot understand how it would be possible for the performer to conceal a glass filled to the brim, as these are, about his person.

After distributing the glasses, and offering an apology for his inability to treat all present, he pretends to overhear a remark that his audience is not satisfied, and that many think they have been slighted. He states that he will endeavor to comply with the demands of his thirsty audience, and retires to fetch a bottle.

Off the stage he removes his coat and places under his right arm a rubber bag filled with wine. To the bag is attached a rubber pipe with a small metal point, which pipe he holds next to his right arm and replaces his coat, leaving the metal end just within the cuff.

The bottle has a small hole in the side, near the bottom, of such a size as to fit the metal point on the rubber pipe. In rinsing the bottle the performer keeps one finger over the hole, thus preventing the

Fig. 58. The Miraculous Wine Bottle.

audience discovering that the bottle differs from an ordinary one. In rinsing the bottle the outside has become wet, and in drying it with a cloth the performer places the metal point on the rubber pipe in the hole in the side of the bottle, thus making connections with the bag of wine. By holding the bottle well down toward the neck, and close to his wrist, he can venture among the audience without fear of detection.

By pressing the right arm against his side the bag is compressed, forcing the wine through the pipe into the bottle.

The glasses are of special make and of very thick glass, making quite a bulky appearance, but of very limited capacity. An assistant carries a tray containing one hundred of the glasses.

The "Mysterious Vase."

Tricks performed with ink and water have always been favorites with magicians, and they have devised means of keeping this trick fully abreast of the times, thus retaining its popularity. The manner of performing the latest ink trick involves such novel principles as to

Fig. 59. The "Mysterious Vase."

puzzle even those who are well posted on modern magic. The "Mysterious Vase" has been presented by but few prestidigitateurs, and the secret so well guarded that comparatively few people know how it is done. (Fig. 59.)

The attention of the audience is called to a glass vase that is filled with water which is resting on a light stand. This vase resembles a large octagon celery glass. In the vase there are a few cut flowers, which the performer removes as he calls attention to the vase and the clear water it contains. The flowers are given to the ladies in the audience, as they have no further connection with the trick.

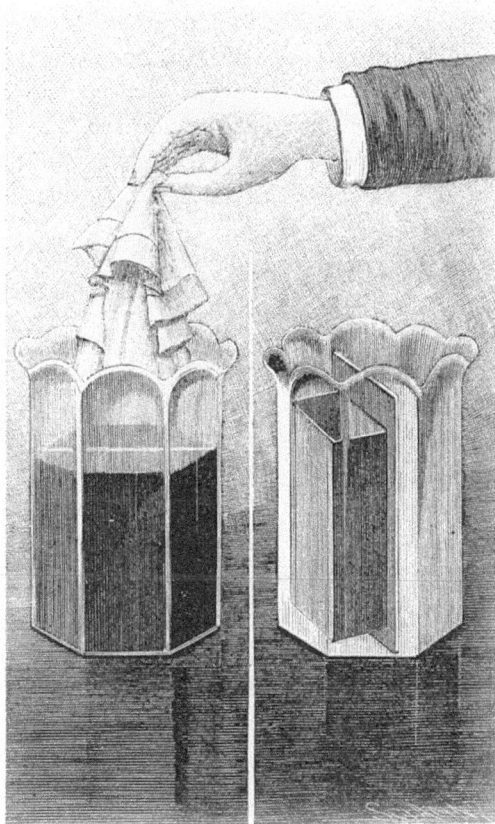

Fig. 60. The Illusion Explained.

A lady's handkerchief is borrowed and the vase covered with it for a moment. On removing the handkerchief, the water that was seen in the vase appears to have changed to ink. While this rapid transformation is very startling, yet the most marvelous part of the trick is to come. The magician bares his forearm, that the audience may see that his sleeves have no connection with the trick, and then proceeds to remove from the ink in the vase six silk handkerchiefs and two lighted candles, each article being perfectly dry.

The means by which this seeming impossibility is performed are as simple as the trick is mysterious, as the following will show. In the center of the vase, reaching from side to side and from the bottom to within a half inch of the top, is a piece of polished mirror. The side edges of the mirror rest in the angles of the vase, and as the vase is only seen from the front, the edges are not seen. The front half of the vase being reflected in the mirror leaves the impression that one is looking directly through the vase, when in reality you only see one-half of the inside. (Fig. 60.)

To the back of this mirror is attached a watertight tin box, in which are placed six small silk handkerchiefs and two candles. The exterior of the box and back of the mirror are painted a dead black color. Enough water is poured into the vase to reach the top edge of the mirror. In the water is dissolved a small portion of iron protosulphate. A few cut flowers are placed in the vase, which is then placed on the stand with the mirror side to the audience, and the candles lighted.

After the flowers are removed and a handkerchief borrowed, the magician secures possession of and palms between his fingers a small lozenge made of pyrogallic acid, which he drops in the water in front of the mirror in the act of covering the vase with the handkerchief. In a very few moments the lozenge dissolves, and the pyrogallic acid of which it is composed causes the water, which holds in solution the iron protosulphate, to change to a good black ink.

On removing the handkerchief with which the vase was covered, ink is seen to have taken the place of the water, and from the center of the vase the performer removes the silk handkerchiefs and candles.

Our first engraving shows the vase of water on the stand; the second shows the vase after the water has changed to ink, with the magician removing one of the silk handkerchiefs. The third illustration represents the vase with one side broken away, showing attached to the back of the mirror the tin receptacle that contains the handkerchiefs and candles.

The "Mermaid's Head."

M. Alber, the prestidigitateur, describes in *La Nature* a variant of a trick which, although old in principle, has recently been brought out in a new and attractive form.

Fig. 61. The "Mermaid's Head."

Upon a light tripod placed in an alcove or recess hung with some sort of a red fabric, such as cotton velvet, stands an aquarium in which gold fish are observed swimming about, and in the center of which is seen a living female head that moves, smiles, and seems to be absolutely at its ease, although deprived of a body and immersed in water. A reference to the figure will show how the apparatus is arranged.

The tripod consists of three gilded copper rods fixed at the bottom to a triangular platform and supporting at the top another platform of nickel-plated metal. At their point of union the three rods, which are firmly brazed to each other, seem to be united by a simple ribbon tied with a bow knot.

From the base to the ribbon there is an empty space, but above the latter there are fixed between the rods three triangular glass mirrors backed with thin and resistant steel plate. The nickel-plated top is movable. Previous to the entrance of the spectators, the woman whose head is to appear, places herself between the mirrors, crosses her legs and rests upon her heels. It is impossible for the apparatus to topple over, since it is firmly screwed to the floor. The nickel-plated top, which is in two pieces, embraces the neck so closely, when put in place, that the joint can scarcely be seen at a short distance. Since the mirrors reflect the floor, which is covered like the walls, it seems as if it were the back of the alcove that is visible between the rods at the upper part; and the entire apparatus appears to be absolutely open.

As for the aquarium trick, that is simple. The aquarium is an adaptation of one that has long been found in the market, and in which are perceived birds that seem to be flying about in the water amid fishes.

The crystal glass aquarium, which is manufactured especially for the purpose, consists of two receptacles. The central one of these is open at the bottom to receive the head, while the outer one is open at the top and contains the water and fishes. As the glass is exceedingly transparent, it is almost impossible to detect the empty space in the center.

The aquarium is placed upon four small nickel-plated supports that permit of the introduction of air into the internal receptacle. The position of the decapitated woman is an exceedingly cramped one, and it is therefore necessary for her to make her exit from the tripod between each exhibition in order to take a well-earned rest.

"Card Cricket."

One of the most effective and pretty tricks performed by the celebrated English magician Mr. Devant is known as "Card Cricket." In this trick the performer shows his hands empty, and takes a pack of cards and requests three ladies to take one card each, and to remember what the cards are. The cards are then replaced in the pack,

Fig. 62. "Card Cricket."

which is well shuffled and cut by one of the audience. The performer then passes for inspection an ordinary cricket bat, which, on its return, he places on a table in full sight of all. He then asks if any one in the audience can bowl, and requests the gentleman who can, to come and have a game of cricket.

Fig. 63. "Card Cricket."

The performer now asks the gentleman to take the pack of cards and bowl at him, and he will be the player or one at the wicket. The performer picks up the bat and says "Play." The cards are bowled at him, and he hits the pack with the bat as the cards are in the air, and, to the astonishment of the audience, the chosen cards are seen sticking to the bat. This very pretty card trick is quite simple to work.

In selecting the cards the ladies were under the impression that they exercised their own free will, but such was not the case. The pack of cards was what is known to magicians as a forcing pack, that is, consisting of only three cards, which, for convenience sake, we will say are the ace of clubs, five of hearts, and nine of spades, one-third of the pack being composed of only one of these cards. The pack being thus made up, it is very easy for a skillful performer to present to the first lady the portion of the pack containing only ace of clubs, to the second lady the part consisting solely of five of hearts, and to the third lady the part that contains only nine of spades. By using such a forcing pack the performer is sure to have the proper cards selected. While the ladies are examining their cards the performer steps to his table on some pretense and slyly changes the forcing pack for an ordinary one consisting of the usual cards, with the exception of the five of hearts, ace of clubs, and nine of spades. This pack he hands to some member of the audience and requests them to have replaced the selected cards and shuffled.

The cricket bat is an ordinary one, which, after being examined by the audience, is laid on a table until the performer finds a gentleman who will bowl the pack at him.

In this simple act of laying the bat on the table we find the principal secret of the trick.

Previous to beginning the performance the magician has placed face down on the table, in a line with each other, an ace of clubs, five of hearts, and nine of spades. The back of each of these cards is lined with cloth similar to the covering of the table, thus preventing any one noticing the cards when placed face down on the table. On the cloth covering of each of the cards is smeared a dab of soft adhesive wax. In placing the bat on the table, care is taken to lay it directly over the three cards, the wax on the backs adhering tightly to the bat.

After the gentleman who has consented to bowl the pack of cards at the performer is in place, the performer picks up the bat, steps back a few feet, and says "Play." The instant the flying cards touch the bat the performer turns it over, bringing into view the side of the bat to which the three cards are sticking, which appear to have been caught on the bat from the flying cards.

Until the pack of cards are thrown against the bat, the magician exercises the greatest care not to turn the side of the bat to which the cards are sticking toward the spectators. Properly presented, this trick has proved most illusive.

"Cupid Lighter than a Butterfly."

The pleasing trick which forms the subject of our engravings owes its success to the ingenious application of mechanical principles. The magician presents for inspection to the audience a large pair of balance scales. The audience is allowed to examine the various parts of the balance before it is erected on the stage. It consists of a central column and a beam resting on a knife-edge, and two pans suspended

Fig. 64. "Cupid Lighter than a Butterfly."

by cords or chains. After the column has been put in position, the beam is put on and a pin inserted, thus making a center for the beam to work on. A gentleman is asked to stand in one of the scale pans,

and then weights are gradually placed in the other pan until his exact
weight is ascertained. The weights are removed, and the gentleman
steps down off the stage. The audience is now convinced that the
scale is to all intents and purposes like the ordinary balance which is
so much used in groceries for weighing tea, coffee, etc., although, of
course, in the present instance, it is built on a mammoth scale.

Fig. 65. The Illusion Explained.

The magician now goes on to say that he will prove the old assertion that "love is lighter than a butterfly" to be absolutely true. He
introduces a little boy dressed as Cupid, with wings and a bow and a

quiver of arrows. When the child steps on the scale pan, it immediately sinks to the floor by his weight. The conjurer now takes a butterfly, and, asking all to direct their attention to the scale, drops it on the opposite pan, which immediately descends to the floor, at the same time raising the pan with the Cupid high in the air. If he takes the butterfly off, the Cupid descends, and every time the prestidigitateur replaces the butterfly, Cupid is raised off the floor.

The trick depends for success upon a carefully devised and concealed mechanism. The balance beam is devoid of any preparation, but the mechanism is cleverly concealed in the column, and motion is imparted to the beam by means of a shaft and bevel gears. The hole in the beam is not perfectly round; it is slightly oval, but not enough so to be easily seen by a casual glance. The pin is also oval, instead of round, and it is made to fit tightly. It will be seen that, when this pin is rocked or tilted, the beam is moved, carrying one scale pan up and the other down. The top of the column is of considerable size, and one side of it is cut away to admit of a bevel gear, which also has an oval hole the same as the beam. When the balance is put together and the beam is placed in position, the oval pin passes through the bevel gear and the beam, forming a horizontal shaft. This vertical wheel meshes with a horizontal gear wheel, which is also secured in the head of the pedestal. A shaft runs through it to the space below the floor, where it terminates in a lever secured at right angles. The magician's assistant, under the stage, grasps the lever, and, pulling it back and forth, transmits a seesaw motion to the beam through the medium of the shaft, the two bevel gears, and the oval pin.

The trick depends very largely for success upon the apparent willingness of the prestidigitateur to allow all parts of the apparatus to be examined, and, as the gear wheels are very cleverly concealed, there is almost no chance of the trick being discovered.

INDEX.